Creative Ways To Start Creative Writing

Volumes One, Two and Three

by

Jessica Grace Coleman

Published by Darker Times

Stafford, UK
www.darkertimes.co.uk

Paperback Edition September 2015

Creative Ways To Start Creative Writing

Volumes One, Two and Three

by

Jessica Grace Coleman

Darker Times Publishing

Also Available From Jessica Grace Coleman

Little Forest Series

The Former World

Memento Mori

The Exalted

Carnival Masquerade

The Gloaming

Short Story Collections

Grown By The Wicked Moon

Non-Fiction

Creative Ways To Start Creative Writing

Volumes 1, 2 & 3

To all the writers and would-be writers out there,
this is for you

Table of Contents

Creative Ways To Start Creative Writing

Volume One

by

Jessica Grace Coleman

Introduction

I love writing. I think I always have. I've always been a big reader, anyway, and I remember the first time I tried to write a novel. I think I must have been about twelve, and I sat down at the family computer (back in those days we only had one between the four of us – perish the thought!) and opened a Word document. I had no idea what I wanted to write about, and I think I spent the first few 'writing' sessions faffing about with the layout settings, getting two pages on the screen so it looked like a proper book, and then figuring out how to set the password up on the document so no one else who used the shared computer (my parents and my brother) would be able to accidentally stumble onto my awful, awful novel. I was very paranoid about this, and I still am today: I hate the idea of anyone reading anything I've written before I've finished it – I feel like I have to justify all the crap bits, saying I'm going to sort them out at the end, and I panic that I haven't read it through a million times yet so I don't know if it actually works or not. Plus, all my first drafts are usually nothing more than extended notes and out of order ideas that may or may not make any sense, and no one needs to see that.

I think I wrote about three pages in the end (if that), and those three pages were about a person pulling up to an old, abandoned house (which in my mind was basically my own house, but as if it was old and decayed – I obviously wasn't very imaginative back then). This person then stupidly entered the house and started to explore, knowing there was something in there but not knowing what it was. I didn't know either – I also hadn't figured out how planning worked at that point – but I never wrote any more of it so I didn't even find out. About twelve years after that, I started writing what would eventually become *The Former World* (the first novel in my young adult paranormal mystery series), although that went much better – I finished it, at least, so that was an improvement. I also planned it a bit too, so I suppose my earlier dabbling in novels taught me something.

Since then I've written four more books in that series (the Little Forest series), a short story collection, and these three volumes on creative writing. I have approximately a gazillion other books in the works, with my next projects being the sixth book in the Little Forest series (*The Vanished*), a new novel in a new series (*The Starling: A Darkford Chronicles Book*), and a new YA sci-fi trilogy starting with *The Downfall*. I am lucky enough to have a full time job involving writing (I run Coleman Editing, where me and my trusty team of writers edit and proofread a whole range of stuff), and although it can be difficult to get on with my own writing after spending hours looking at other people's, I've found that it's become much easier over the years.

Why? Well, like I learnt things from my first attempt at novel writing (which, as you already know, was a complete disaster), I've also learnt a lot from the last few years. A lot of that stuff is rather boring technical stuff about self-publishing, and while I do delve into some of those things in these three volumes, my main focus is on getting into the creative writing mode in the first place. This is what I find most difficult about writing; once I'm into a novel, I love it, and can't wait to get it finished, but the actual sitting down and starting it? Well, it's pretty much akin to a nightmare involving giant spiders and horrifying clowns. It's a mental block, but knowing that never seems to help – I know I can physically sit down and start writing, but my mind prevents me from doing it. I'm not saying I hear condescending voices in my head saying, 'You'll never finish this manuscript so why even bother trying? You're a rubbish writer and you'll never get anywhere!' but there's just something that tries to stop me, every single time. You may have experienced this too, and if you haven't, you're very, very lucky!

As this was happening to me every time I tried to start writing a book, I began to try different things to get me in the writing zone, and while some didn't work at all, others did. I started doing these things – and variations of these things – more often, and soon I knew exactly what to do if I sat down and got that evil mental block. I'd go over my list of activities and techniques to get me in the zone, and I'd pick whichever one I felt like most at that moment. Soon I was sitting down and typing away without any of the old doubts flooding my brain, something that has done wonders for my productivity (and my attitude to self-publishing).

Now, I feel I should put a bit of a disclaimer here: some of the ideas in this book are silly, strange, and perhaps not the kind of thing you're used to reading about if you've devoured other books on writing, but I believe that thinking outside the box when it comes to getting creative is far more important than trying to stick to traditional methods and techniques (although of course, for some people the traditional methods will be the only thing they need). And if you're a creative person – which, as a writer, is pretty much a given – then thinking outside the box should come naturally to you. This book is fun in its approach, but serious in its intent: I want to help you get into the creative mindset, and to get you writing creatively. Hopefully you'll appreciate the fact that some of the ideas to get you into this mindset are fun and quirky, and perhaps it will change the way you view planning and preparing to write your novel/short story/whatever it is you're trying to do. Writing is fun, and while many people hate the planning and 'getting in the zone' parts, we can make them fun too. You just need to give yourself permission to try out a few things and see what works for you. Take control of your mind and stop suffering from those mental blocks and those terrifying, paralysing self-doubts.

This book isn't about the process of self-publishing or of trying to find an agent or publisher (although I do mention these briefly), as there are already so many great books out there on this topic that will give you the information you need. Personally, I self-publish all of my books and I really enjoy the creative freedom that indie publishing gives you; now I enjoy every single part of the writing process, from coming up with an idea, to fleshing that idea out, to plotting and planning, to writing, editing, and finally, releasing my work out onto the world and hiding away until I get my first good review. With this in mind, I've collated various ideas of how to start writing that book, whether you're a first time novelist or an established author who finds it difficult to get going on a new project. I really hope you enjoy these books, and I hope you put aside the time to try out at least some of these ideas, even if you don't think they'll work. They've worked for me, and they can work for you too – just give it a go; what have you got to lose?

Now, I know what some of you are probably thinking: 'I barely have any free time to write, let alone read these books and try out a load of techniques', but if you want to be a writer, you have to put the work in, and if you're reading this, you obviously want to do that. Just to recap, I have so far written five books in the Little Forest paranormal series, featuring Beth Powers and her normal (and not so normal) struggles in a small village in England, as well as the short story collection, *Grown By The Wicked Moon*, featuring 14 weird and wonderful tales. I am also in the process of writing the sixth book in the Little Forest series, *The Vanished*, as well as my second short story collection, *Midnight Remains*. I'm in the first draft stages of *The Downfall* – the first in a sci-fi trilogy for Young Adults – as well as being in the planning stages of *The Starling*, book one in The Darkford Chronicles. Throw in these three books on creative writing and my own business editing and ghostwriting, and I'm pretty busy. But I make the time to get on with my own writing, no matter what.

If you're a morning person (which I most definitely am not), get up an hour earlier and do an hour a day of writing. You'll be done by breakfast, and those 7 hours a week will really start to add up. If you're like me, stay up an hour later and get your work done before bed (but perhaps not *just* before bed, as looking at screens before sleep is most definitely not a good idea for your brain). If you want to be a writer, you'll find the time to write, and in order to get writing you have to be in the correct mindset, otherwise those 7 hours a week won't be very productive, and you'll be wasting time instead of making the most of it. Think of reading these books and trying out some of these ideas as a sort of investment in your writing future; if you can get to the point where you sit down and are immediately motivated to write, those 7 hours a week will be the best hours you spend in terms of planning for your future (especially if you want to make money from your writing).

I love the creative parts of planning and writing a story or a novel, but I also have to put my business hat on and deal with all of the administrative elements of my business, so in the past I've found it hard to distinguish between the two roles I have to play – one wearing my creative hat and one wearing the less stylish and slightly boring admin hat. You may have something similar in your life, juggling your need to be creative with your duties of looking after your family, or juggling several jobs with your desire to write. It's all about striking up a balance, and the quicker and easier you can get into the creative mindset when you want to write, the more you'll be able to achieve (and maintain) this balance.

This book is going to be several things in one – some tips on how to start thinking about writing, some recommendations for apps and programs that will help you on your way, and – hopefully – a kick up the arse that so many writers (including me) often need. I know how hard it is to start a creative project, to get into that creative zone and to ignore everything else (all the real world stuff) that's going on around you. I've been there, and I've been there so many times that I've found a whole heap of different ways to get myself into that zone, some of which can be really fun.

The idea with the books in this series is to get you to the point where you not only *can* sit down and write, but where you *can't wait* to get writing, whether you're writing a short story, a novel, a series of novels, or anything else. If you try and write creatively when you're not in the creative zone, you'll quickly get bored, give up hope, and possibly stop altogether. Especially if you generally think of your normal everyday life as being quite mundane, it can seem like a huge challenge to get into the headspace of a creative person. But if you're a writer – and you're a writer whether you publish your work or not – you have the potential to get into that headspace, no matter what is going on around you or what 'real life' incidents are currently taking place. What's brilliant about reading is that you get to step out of your real life for a few hours and put on someone else's shoes, and when it comes to writing, this escape from reality is even better, because *you* get to write that reality. You have creative freedom – something you may not be fortunate enough to have in your day job – and this is where you can really let your imagination run riot.

As I've already mentioned (and as you're probably beginning to realise), I love writing. I love everything about it: coming up with storylines, making a wide range of characters, and creating entire worlds for them to live in. I also love the process of self publishing: designing a cover (with help!), writing the blurb and the sales description, then putting it out there for readers to instantly get their hands on. It's what I'm passionate about, but when I first started writing, I found it very hard to get into the right mindset, to get 'in the zone' as many people say. I think it goes back to my school days – and then my Uni days. Although I love writing, the thought of sitting down and writing an essay on something I had no interest in was really not my idea of fun, and I'd put it off for as long as I could. Even though I'm writing (more or less) what I want these days, it's still hard to shake that mindset off when it's been drummed into you over several years.

There's just something about sitting down in front of a computer and staring at a blank page that makes me freeze. I get overcome with self-doubt, and I start questioning myself before I've even begun: why am I doing this? Why am I even bothering to start if the odds of me actually finishing this thing are so low? No one's going to read it (or like it) anyway, so I may as well not even try. These kinds of negative feelings and doubts don't just apply to writing, as I'm sure you know – they can rear their ugly head during any day-to-day activity. Applying for a new job, looking at houses you can't afford, getting up out of that armchair and going for a run... we all get bombarded with these feelings sometimes, but it's how we respond to these negative emotions that define the outcome. I've so far written five novels in my Little Forest paranormal mystery series, but if I gave up after I sat down to write the very first one – which I nearly did, several times – I never would have found out how much I enjoy writing, and in turn, self-publishing. You just need to get over those initial hurdles, those initial niggling doubts, and that's what this book is all about.

So, some of the techniques and ideas in this book you may have heard of already, whereas others are more unique notions that I've come up with simply to get those creative juices flowing. No matter how strange some of these ideas seem, you'll never know until you try them. I'll be using examples throughout regarding how I've used these techniques to fuel the ideas in my own books, and I'll also put in as many links and resources as I can to help you out. These are also listed in the 'Resources' section at the end of the book for easy access, so there's no excuse not to try at least some of the following methods. I'm also including several appendices in each book so you can easily flick to (or click to) some of the ideas in this series, some of which are repeated from the main text and some of which are extra information/ideas/examples of things I've mentioned in the books. There's also an 'easy to read list of creative techniques' for after you've read the books and want to double check some of the ideas without reading through everything again. My aim with these books is to help you get into the creative mindset, but it's also about making this as easy as possible for you to do.

So what are you waiting for? The sooner you get reading, the sooner you can start getting creative.

***

Please note that I have no affiliations with any of the websites, books or apps I recommend in these books, and I'm not being paid to discuss any of them. They are simply things I've used (or things my friends have used and enthused to me about) that I think may help you in your quest to get in the creative writing zone. If I seem to favour some more than others it is only because I have more experience of using them, and I don't want to give you any incorrect information by going into detail over something I've never tried. I hope you'll find the resources in these books useful.

Starting Out

Starting any writing project can be tricky (which is what these three volumes of books are all about), but before we start looking at the various techniques and activities you can try to attempt getting in the zone, there are a few things we need to look at, understand, and get over. We're going to start with two words that cause some writers to go cold, some to stop in their tracks, and others to run away screaming: writer's block.

Writer's Block

Ah yes, the infamous writer's block. For some authors, it is the bane of their lives, while others will swear blind that it doesn't exist. I place myself somewhere in the middle of those two extremes. I believe it is a definite, genuine thing, but that writer's block isn't perhaps the right term. I think of it as more of a mental block, one that we can – and do – get in many different areas of our lives. These mental blocks often occur when we are stressed or when we don't believe we can actually achieve what we want to achieve, and for me personally I'm reminded of homework, especially when it was in subjects I didn't particularly like. If I got it into my head

– before I'd even sat down to do the work – that I couldn't do it, it would take me forever to get over that mental block and make myself believe that I actually *could* do it. It is like a literal block of wood in my brain, not something that stops my thoughts getting through altogether, but one that slows the process down considerably as I have to hack my way through it first. (Of course, a literal block of wood in your head would have far more devastating consequences, but let's not worry about that right now!)

This mental blockage always reminds me of one of Derren Brown's TV shows, where he made a woman change her mind on several different things (supposedly using NLP/tapping techniques). For example, he made her look at the colour of her own car, after having put the wrong colour in her head: she swore blind it was black when really it was red, and it took just seconds for Derren to reprogramme her brain. Before he did this, he retuned her brain regarding another idea, this time with the homework she had yet to complete and her worries about not achieving good results at school. The fear had seemed like such a monumental thing to her that she was having difficulty even wrapping her head around it, but after a magical mental unblocking from Derren, she suddenly found the idea of achieving her academic goals to be no problem at all – she couldn't understand what she'd been so worried about. This illustrated just how changeable our minds can be, and when we think we can't do something, we just need to look at it from a different perspective and get rid of our mind blocks (and perhaps try some tapping!). This is what I hope will happen when you try at least some of the techniques in these books.

Starting a book is hard; no matter what kind of book it is – novel, autobiography, memoir, non-fiction – the beginning is always extremely difficult. There's no getting around it. Some people love to plan every single second of their novel before they even write down the first word, while others jump in and wing it right to the very end, but either way, you've still got to get to the point where you can sit down and start writing, and that is never easy.

Like I said, personally, I find the start of a book incredibly hard to get into. I stare at a blank word document and it takes me right back to having to write essays at school – something I hated with a fiery passion, no matter what the topic. This carried on into university, with me sitting in a different room in a different house in a different city, but still staring at that same blank word document and wondering what on earth I was going to write.

Fortunately, now that I've tried so many different things, a blank word document no longer puts the fear of God into me. I look at that blank page and know that soon it will be filled with words. Maybe not brilliant words – not straight away, at least – but words, nonetheless. It's nothing to freak out about. I've changed the way I think about it, and it no longer feels like a monumental, unachievable task. This is what we all need to do, and these books could be the starting point for you.

Visualisation

This idea won't be for everyone, but I find it really helps me when I'm feeling tired or when I'm having an attack of the 'can't be bothered's. Basically, it just involves reminding yourself of why you're doing this, whatever your reasons may be – whether you want to be rich and/or famous, if you want to prove to yourself you can write a book, if you want to change your entire lifestyle, or if you simply want to make a bit of cash every month to go towards the bills (none of these are the right or wrong answers, by the way). You can do this with the idea of visualisation.

First of all, you need to know what you're aiming for. Think of the main reason you want to write and then make a note of it somewhere. In my case, I started writing because I wanted to see if I could complete that first novel. I did, and then my reason changed to wanting to see if I could write a sequel. I did that too, and so I had to decide what my new reason was. Once I realised that I could actually write a novel from start to finish, I started setting my sights higher and higher. Now my reason to write is because I want to spend my days doing what I love, instead of getting paid by the hour at some repetitive desk job that's going nowhere. I've had several retail and admin jobs over the years, and the idea of being able to do my own writing full-time was one of the biggest motivations I could think of. I had no desire to be ridiculously wealthy or famous, but I really wanted a lifestyle change – to spend my days doing what I love, and to make enough money from it to live. You need to find your own primary motivation, whatever that may be.

Once you've decided why you're doing this, try and visualise it. Picture yourself handing out paperback copies of your book to friends and family, talking about your work on a local radio show, or living the flexible lifestyle of a full-time writer. If money is part of your aim (and if it is, there's no shame in it!), picture yourself in that big beautiful house, or in that brand new car, being able to provide for your family without working yourself into the ground every week. Whatever it is, picture it as clearly as you can, and think back to that mental image whenever you feel like giving up, or whenever you receive a bad review, or whenever someone tries to put you or your dream down. Now that you've got something to aim for, focusing on the task at hand should be so much easier, and if it's not, perhaps spend some more time visualising that perfect outcome!

If you're finding the idea of visualising your future self a little vague and difficult to do, how about visualising your perfect day in this future? Instead of dragging yourself out of bed and commuting into a job you hate, coming home knackered and doing nothing but watching TV all night, picture yourself leaping out of bed, perhaps eating something healthy or doing a spot of exercise (a morning walk out in the fresh air) before coming back in, getting a cup of tea, and sitting down to write. Imagine yourself opening emails from your fans, reading great reviews of your books, looking at your sales and finding some money in your bank thanks to readers who've bought your novels. Imagine yourself writing your next bestseller, working to your own timescales and deadlines and not having to put up with a boss who rushes your work and yells at you for coming in late or spending too much time in the kitchen getting your tea. Imagine finishing work for the day and curling up with a book, a legitimate 'procrastiworking' exercise that is not only relevant but necessary for your career! By the way, the whole time you're doing this, you're living in your perfect house with everything you need to continue and thrive in your chosen career – a career you love. OK, so that might be a rather idealised version of the future, but so what? Use it to motivate yourself, and who knows? If you work very, very hard, all of that might come true.

Of course, not everyone will be able to (or want to) do this, or be able to take anything from it – sometimes we need something more concrete to grasp onto, more solid than just an idea in our heads. If this is you, no problem; there are other ways we can take the idea of visualisation and mould it into something we can use for inspiration. More of that later.

Procrastiworking

You've probably already heard of this term, but if not, you may want to add it to your vocabulary. It basically means putting off working on your main project by working on something else, or not doing what you're supposed to be doing in favour of doing things that will help you when you *do* come to do what you're supposed to be doing. Did that make sense?! You're not procrastinating, you're procrastiworking, which sounds so much better, doesn't it?

I do this a lot, and it's much better than full-on procrastination, as even if you're not writing your novel, you can be doing things towards writing it, which however way you think of it, can't be a waste of time. By starting slowly and procrastiworking your way to your big project, you're giving your brain the chance to get into that creative headspace without freaking it out straight away.

17

Here are some things you can do to procrastiwork your way to writing that novel:

Research: Are you writing a detailed historical novel, or perhaps a murder mystery where you need to know about police procedure? In that case, you'll need to do a lot of research in order to make your book realistic. Actually, no matter what you're writing, you'll probably need to do at least some research for parts of the book, and understanding the subjects you're going to write about can help get you inspired.

Reading: Ah, the easiest form of procrastiworking there is. If you're writing a book in a particular genre, it makes sense to read other books in that genre, especially recent books that have done well in the current market. This, in fact, is a form of research, so it definitely comes under procrastiworking. Just make sure you don't subconsciously steal any ideas from the books you're reading!

Planning: Not everyone plans their novel out in great detail, but I mention a lot of different ways of planning and plotting in these creative writing books, and some of them can be far more fun than just sitting and typing up your outline. Any type of planning – no matter how you do it – is worthwhile, but the sillier, more fun ideas can definitely fall into the category of procrastiworking.

Reading writer resources, interviews and books on writing: These are listed elsewhere in the three volumes, and they definitely come under procrastiworking – learning as much as you can about writing and the industry will really help when you come to getting your book published, and reading about the success of others is a great motivator.

Creating your author website: This is a great way to procrastiwork, as it's something that needs doing at some point – and the sooner the better. People will want to look you up if they like your books, and if you don't have a nice, finished website ready for them, they might forget about you and look elsewhere for their new favourite writer. Creating your own website (if you don't already have one) can be a brilliant way to get motivated; as you see all the pages coming together, you won't be able to wait until your 'books' page is filled with titles, or until your mailing list has hundreds if not thousands of people signed up to it. It's another way of visualising the outcome you want, and designing websites can be fun too!

Ignoring Other People

This may sound rather simple – and rather rude – but sometimes, you just have to be a little selfish if you want to get writing. This can be harder or easier depending on your living situation, of course – it's always going to be more difficult when you work a full-time job then come home to a large household, with someone always wanting to speak to you or spend time with you – but it can be done. In fact, it needs to be done if you're serious about following your passion, and if you're reading this, then I guess you must be. Even if it's just for half an hour every evening, get your family used to the idea that you'll be shutting yourself away (wherever you can – the spare room, the garage, a closet), and that you don't want to be disturbed under any circumstances (unless, you know, there's an actual emergency).

Turn your phone off, put in earplugs if you need them, and shut yourself off from the world. It can be hard to get in the zone if you only have a set number of minutes a day to do it, but with practice, it is possible. And once your family realise that you are actually serious about 'this whole writing thing', they're more likely to give you the time you need to get on with it. You might feel bad to start with, but remember that in the long run, it will be a good thing. People who pursue their passion – who actually do it instead of just thinking about it, planning it, and daydreaming about it – generally tend to be happier, and a happier you will mean a happier family. So really, ignoring them for a few minutes a day is a good thing. Plus, it might get you out of washing the dishes or feeding the dog.

Dealing With People's Initial Reactions

It's sad but true that when you tell people you're writing a novel, you'll get a lot of different reactions, and not all of them will be good. Now, don't get me wrong, most people will be supportive – they'll be excited to read it, and they'll ask you all kinds of questions about how you're writing a book, because they've always wanted to do it themselves. It can be quite a nice feeling, having people so excited, but it can also put a lot of pressure on you: what if you don't actually finish it? What if you do and your family and friends don't like it? What if they hate it but they're too nice to say anything to your face? What then? As usual, doubts and fears will start to enter your mind, but you'll soon get used to this if you carry on writing, and you'll soon learn to ignore them completely.

It's the other people that you need to prepare yourself for – the ones who'll act insanely surprised when you say you're writing a novel, or who'll frown at the very thought, or who – worst of all – will start laughing. This can be a little off-putting, sure (I mean, it's not like you've just told them you're an alien from outer space or anything), but if you're prepared for it happening, it won't have much of an effect on you. Sometimes people are jealous (they wish they had the guts to sit down and write a book), sometimes people will just be caught off guard (most people they know don't write books, after all), and some really won't believe that you're actually going to do it. They'll say all the right things and nod and smile, but you'll be able to tell that they don't really believe you. That's fine – you have your own doubts about your writing ability, so why shouldn't other people?

You can turn this into a positive thing, however; it's these people who you'll be able to think of when you're sitting at your computer, looking for inspiration. So your great aunt Gladys – will all the best intentions in the world – doesn't think you'll be able to finish one chapter, let alone a whole book? Take that negativity and use it, fuel that motivational fire and get the job done. She'll probably be delighted to be proven wrong, and you can inform her that she had a hand in your writing!

Generally, you'll have to deal with these kinds of things before you even publish anything, although there is a way around it – keep your writing a secret. There's a bit of a thrill in doing this, as every time you sit down to write you can do it safe in the knowledge that no one has any idea you're writing a book – and the looks of surprise on their faces when you produce your finished manuscript can also be a brilliant motivational tool. Be careful, though: if you don't live alone and are constantly squirrelling yourself away in your room to write, people may start to come to their own conclusions about what you're doing..!

Money

I think it's at least worth mentioning money in a book like this, because as much as we hate to admit it to other people, money is usually a motivator, in at least some small way. Most indie writers realise that they'll never get rich or famous from their own writing – although you've got to dream big to be big! – but it can help to think about money to a certain extent.

There are plenty of self-published writers out there who make a comfortable living from their books, and if that's what you're aiming for, great! Having a goal – even a monetary one – is a good way to keep motivated. Of course, a lot of writers consider themselves as 'artists' and resign themselves to the fact that they probably won't be appreciated in their own lifetime, but things are changing, publishing is changing, and it's getting easier and easier to make money from books without going down the traditional publishing route. It won't be easy, but if you have the self-belief and the discipline to sit down and write a novel from start to finish, you have all the tools you need to start making money from your writing (as long as you continue to sit down and write more novels from start to finish – hardly anyone is going to make any money from just one book).

So, money can be a good motivator, but don't rely on it, and don't think that it's going to be easy. You need to love writing first, and think about the money you may or may not make afterwards. The feeling of getting your own book out there and into the hands of the buying public can be just as – if not more – rewarding, and if your writing is good and your marketing is effective, the sales will come. You just need to believe in yourself, and work your arse off (but if you love writing as much as you think you do, it won't really feel like 'work', not in the mundane 9-5 office way, anyway).

Research

This can turn into a massive procrastiworking session (or sessions) but most books involve research of some kind, and often – as well as giving you the info you need – it can also inspire you. This is why it's not procrastination but procrastiworking, which is almost as good as working, as at least you feel like you're getting somewhere with your project.

If you're writing a crime drama, this can involve looking up past criminal cases or unsolved mysteries, reading eyewitness accounts and transcripts from real court proceedings, or understanding the justice system and how prisons operate. If you're writing fiction, you don't have to be exact (the great thing about fiction is you can make things up), but there is a line – you don't want to come off sounding like you don't know what you're writing about, and if your book is primarily based in a courtroom and you know nothing about how courts work, your reader is going to be able to tell (especially if they love court room dramas and actually know more than you do).

Generally, the more info you have, the more realistic your book will be, and the more inspiration you're likely to get. Better yet, if you can, find a real person to talk to about the subject in question, even if it's just tracking down a subject matter expert or blogger on the Internet and sending them a message. They'll probably be flattered to be asked, you'll get some juicy info, and everyone will end up happy. Give them an acknowledgement in the book and they'll be even happier. You might know someone (or know someone who knows someone) who can help you out in 'real life' too – are you writing about the police but have never been involved with them? See if any of your friends or family know someone who work on the force, and the same with council workers, hospital workers, and anything else that may be relevant to your book.

If, for example, you're writing a book where one of the characters is on the reception of a busy hospital, you can learn a lot from talking to – you've guessed it – someone who works on the reception of a busy hospital. They're bound to have seen a lot of weird and wonderful things over the years, and although they'd have to stick to patient confidentiality and so on, they can be a great source of information – both in terms of practicalities and hospital procedures, as well as in terms of the kinds of patients they have to deal with on a daily basis. Inject some real life into your books and your readers will love you for it.

Self-Belief

Now, I don't want to go too far down the self-help route in this book, but I think it's worth mentioning at least a little bit, as the way you approach anything in life can make all the difference. If you wake up in the morning and think you're going to have a rubbish day, then you probably will. If you go into something with nothing but negativity and fear of what could happen or what could go wrong, then you won't get very far, and even if you do, the outcome probably won't be that great. If you think something's going to suck, it probably will.

Here's the problem: no matter how many ideas you have, or how big your writing ambitions are, you absolutely won't get anywhere without believing in yourself. I know this can be hard – I constantly struggle with this too – but in many ways, it's step one to becoming a writer. If you don't truly believe that you're going to finish the novel you're starting (there's a rather depressing statistic that states only a very small percentage of people actually finish a book they start writing), then you probably won't. You'll have that thought in the back of your mind as you write, and if you decide halfway through that you're going to give up, you'll justify it to yourself by saying, 'I never expected to finish this anyway, so I'm just happy I gave it a shot and got this far.' If you really want to be a writer, then you have to believe that you can, no matter how many doubts you're feeling or what 'society' tells you about being an author. Screw all that and write anyway.

Just think of your favourite authors. Many of these will have experienced a lot of rejection over the years, and they probably thought of giving up more than once, but they didn't. They kept on going, taking it one day at a time, and they believed in themselves – because if they didn't, they would have given up ages ago, and you wouldn't have their books on your shelf now. They didn't give up, and neither should you – who knows what the future holds? But you'll only find out if you keep going, no matter what. And of course, if you never even start then you *definitely* won't get anywhere.

Get Positive

These books are all about getting in the right creative headspace in order to start writing, but before you do this you need to get in the right positive mindset. Luckily, this can be done in several ways (some of which will come up in the course of these books as we look at different techniques). If it's your very first attempt at creative writing of any kind, you're probably thinking of how daunting the whole thing is – how the hell does anyone get anything written, let alone an entire book? And that's not even thinking about long-running series and prolific authors who publish a novel a year or more. At first it may seem crazy, but once you take that first step, everything else will get easier. And the more positive you are and the more self-belief you have when you make that first step, the better.

If you're generally a happy, smiley person, getting into a positive mindset won't be hard, but for others, it won't be something that comes naturally at all. First off, you need to change the way you think about writing; if you're thinking of it as 'work', something to suffer through until it's finished, then you're never going to enjoy being a writer, and if you don't enjoy it, what's the point? If you're just doing this for a hobby, you'll find it easier to think of writing as something fun, but if you're eventually planning on making money from it, it can be a little harder to change your point of view. Some of the techniques discussed in these books will help with that, but there are also some simple things you can do to get in the positive headspace:

Exercise: Exercising will get your body feeling great, and that rush of endorphins might be exactly what you need to get yourself and your mind feeling great too. Exercising outside in the fresh air will help even more.

Review Old Work/Compliments on Writing: My guess is that if you want to be a writer, something may have happened in your past to encourage you. Did you do well at English in school? Did you write a story that someone loved? Has someone told you you're a good storyteller or that you have a way with words? Whatever it is, think back over those times and those compliments and let them give you the boost you need to get back in the writing saddle.

Music: I talk about music later on in these books, but I really do believe in the potential for music to alter your mindstate, almost instantly sometimes. Put on some bands or artists that you love, or play some well known, cheesy motivational songs to get you inspired (check out the Creative Playlists section in the appendix for more info).

Research Writing Success Stories: You probably know the stories of how your favourite authors got their publishing deals, but what about more recent, independent writers? Indie publishing (or self-publishing) is getting more and more popular, and websites like Amazon and Createspace are always showcasing the authors who took on self-publishing and won. If you're planning on going down this route, read up on them and start to get excited about your own writing – they did it, and so can you!

Read Your Favourite Book: We all have our favourite novel (or novels, if like me you can never decide on anything), and as an avid reader, you probably love it when you finish a book and immediately feel like you have to read the next in the series, or when you stay up all night just to read the next chapter, then the next chapter, then the next. That feeling – of being absolutely, completely hooked on a story – is a great feeling to have, and by reading your favourite book before you start your big project, you can take that feeling into the writing process for your own book. Plus, just think: one day, someone could get that feeling while reading *your* novel. How great would that be?

Meditation, Mantras and Mindfulness: I mention this in a bit – and there are thousands of books on these subjects – but if you're not in the right headspace, it may be time to try some of these techniques. Take time out to meditate, repeat some positive mantras to yourself, and really become aware and in tune with your body and mind. Filter out all the negatives in your brain and focus on the positives.

Make sure you don't put too much pressure on yourself; no one's expecting you to write a Shakespearean-level manuscript on your first go. Just remember that first drafts are never brilliant, you can work on it during the editing stage, and the more practice you get, the better you'll get at writing. What matters the most is actually sitting down and writing, carrying on even when it feels like the last thing you want to do, and when you finally get to the end of your first ever manuscript, the feeling of achievement and satisfaction will be hard to match. Then again, when you get a physical copy of your book in your hands, that's a pretty great feeling too! The point is, everyone has doubts, but you can't let those doubts control you. If we did that, we'd never do anything in our lives, and we certainly wouldn't attempt anything like writing a book.

Get Rid Of Doubts

If you really do have no self-belief at all, then you need to get some, and quick. There are plenty of books out there on this subject, and plenty of people offering counselling and therapy, but you don't have to spend hundreds or thousands of pounds on getting to the point where you believe in yourself. Until you do something, you have no idea if you can do it or not, and it's the same with writing. Most of it is all in our heads, and a lot of people believe they don't have the skills to write when they've never even tried it in the first place.

Some people write themselves off before they've even given it a go, for a whole host of reasons. For instance, your English teacher at school may have told you you're a bad writer, or another adult may have told you that you'll never amount to anything. Well, if that's the case, then this is your chance to prove them wrong – to show them (and everyone else) what you're capable of, and being able to tell someone that you've written and published a book will no doubt impress them. This isn't a reason to want to write a book, of course, but if you're having trouble believing you can do it, thinking about the people who've put you down in the past can be a great motivator to sit down and create something awesome – just try not to get bogged down in any negativity. We need to keep things positive, remember?

It's worth mentioning that everyone has doubts. Even if you're the most confident person in the world, you can't deny that you have at least some fears and worries about things in your life, whether it's to do with your job, your personal life, your aspirations, or anything else. Life is hard, that's the truth. If we want to achieve anything, we have to work hard; apart from a few lucky people, nothing is handed to us on a plate. The thing is, if what you're working hard at is your passion – say, writing – then it shouldn't feel like work at all. That's not to say you don't have to put the hours in; if you're serious about being a writer and getting your work out there, you should be more than willing to put all of your effort into your dream, no matter how long it takes. It's often just the first step that can be hard to get your head around, but once you've given yourself permission to write a book, and got past all that negative crap whirling around in your head from experiences in the past, you'll find it easier to sit down and write.

Get Excited!

In terms of being an author, we're currently living in one of the most exciting times to be a novel writer. We have more options than ever before when it comes to publishing, and if we go down the self-publishing route, we can have complete creative control over everything. It is a very, very exciting time to be a writer, so get excited! We have so much technology available to us now – so many apps and websites and pieces of software right at our fingertips – and it has never been easier or more fun to publish your own book.

Just think – within a few days of finishing your final draft, you can have your book formatted, a cover designed, and everything uploaded to a website. Within hours your book can be available online for people to buy – as ebooks, as paperbacks, and even as hardbacks (although these are rarer in the self-publishing world and not really needed). Friends and family can purchase your book, and so can complete strangers! Complete strangers from all over the world, no less! It's incredible when you think about it, especially as you don't have to be the best writer in the universe to get your work out there, and you don't have to be in the right place at the right time, with the perfect book for that year's most popular selling genres. You don't have to spend years impressing agents and publishing houses, only to find that you've got nowhere, or that your published book lasted six months on the shelves before it was pulled out due to its poor sales performance.

Getting   published   in   the   traditional   way   isn't impossible, but it does involve jumping through several hoops you might not want to jump through, changing everything from the name and cover of your book to the way you're promoted as an author. Some people (myself included) don't have the time for that. I like writing my books, getting them finished, uploading them to the relevant websites, and having them available online just days later. In this world of instant gratification, it's a brilliant way of getting closure on a project, of feeling satisfied that you've done a good job, and if you happen to get good reviews on those books, even better! The feeling is indescribable, and it's all in your hands – it's within your reach, you just have to go after it.

And if that doesn't get you excited, perhaps the idea of making money from your books will. I'm not saying you'll be an instant millionaire, or that you'll be able to give up your day job (though some indie authors do after a while), but wouldn't it be good to start getting money deposited in your account from Amazon or Createspace or Smashwords, or wherever you're selling your books? Even if it's just a few pounds a month, that's an extra treat you can give yourself, or it could pay for your phone or part of your bills. Every little helps, and once you realise you can start making money (actual money, in your bank, ready to be spent), then you'll start to realise that you can make more – you just need to believe in yourself, and carry on writing.

Doesn't the idea of money in the bank sound exciting to you? That, plus holding your book in your hands, should get you really enthusiastic and motivated, and it is this feeling you need to remember when you start to get that irritating creative block. Unfortunately, we all have to deal with this at one time or another, but as with anything in life, it's how we deal with it that counts.

Mantras

As I mentioned above, one way of drumming some positivity into yourself (if you don't feel too silly doing it, anyway) is to go down the mantra route. Basically, this can involve staring at yourself in the mirror and chanting the same thing over and over again (or if you prefer, 'saying' the same words a few times, if chanting doesn't sound like your kind of thing). It's all about reinforcing the words and making your brain believe them through repetition. Say something enough times, and you'll start to believe it. Sit down and write often enough, and you'll start to believe you can do that too, that you can finish that novel.

Here are a few examples of possible mantras to use when psyching yourself up to write (or just psyching yourself up for the day):

'I can do this' – sweet and short, but effective.
'I am the author of my own life, I am in control of what happens' – write your book, write your life.
'I believe in myself, and I know what I can achieve – I can achieve whatever I put my mind to' – say this until you really believe it!
'I will not worry, for worrying is a huge waste of time. I will stop worrying, stop doubting, and do what needs to be done' – let's get over those self-doubts.
'I am capable, more capable than I give myself credit for' – a lot of people worry about being incapable of achieving their dreams, but these are often the people who don't even bother to try.

So, give yourself a pep talk, tell your friends and family that you ARE going to write a book, get fired up by exercising or reading your favourite novel, and then start. Of course, it's not always as easy as that, and in these books we'll be looking at the many different ways you can get to the point where you're ready to start putting words on that page. Inspiration can be hard to come by, but the ways you can go about chasing that inspiration are almost endless. So what are you waiting for? Let's get inspired and let's get creative!

Self-Publishing Vs. Traditional Publishing

I'm only going to touch briefly on this (because it is a huge topic that would cover many books in itself), but if you're a first time writer, at some point you're going to have to decide what you want to do with your finished book. While there are many different options – including leaving it to rot in a drawer, destroying it because you can't possibly conceive of someone else reading your words, or paying a printer to print a short run for you and your family and no one else – the main ones you'll have to decide between are self-publishing (or 'indie' publishing, as it's often called) and traditional publishing.

I'm going to talk a bit about these here, as I believe that having a plan and knowing where you're going with your writing (what you're going to do with your book once it's finished) can be a really helpful motivational tool, as otherwise you could be writing with no particular aim in sight and therefore no particular reason to keep on going. So, this section may be a little more boring compared to the rest in these books (and if you already know about publishing, feel free to skip ahead), but I believe there is merit in gaining this knowledge before you even start writing. So here we go…

Traditional Publishing

Let's start with the bad news. These days, if you're a first time writer, you'll find it very hard to get one of the large publishing houses interested in you; unless you're already a celebrity or are a subject matter expert writing a non-fiction book on something the market is in desperate need of, you're unlikely to get anywhere with the large publishers. They get an insane amount of submissions each day, and if you don't have a publishing history or an agent, your submission will probably end up in the bin. Sad times, but like with anything in life, if you have your heart set on a traditional publishing contract, you shouldn't let any of this put you off. You haven't been put off writing, have you? So why should you be put off going after your publishing dream?

If you want to go ahead and try and get a publishing deal, there are some things you need to know in advance so that you're prepared when you come to start sending your work out there. Most don't accept unsolicited manuscripts, so the next step you'll have to take in that case is to get yourself an agent, although even that is as far away from a piece of cake as you can get. You'll need a killer, kickass, relevant book in a genre that is easily identifiable and marketable (and 'current' or matching future trends), you'll need an eye-catching cover letter with a reason why your book is going to sell (is it the first in a series? Does it have a unique selling point? Is it based on a true story?), and you'll need to catch that agent's or publisher's eye out of all the hundreds of manuscripts and cover letters they get sent each week. Timing is crucial, good writing is absolutely vital, and unfortunately, luck does seem to play a big part in it. It's tough, but it's the truth. It can be a long, hard slog, and even after years of trying, there's absolutely no guarantee that you'll get published by anyone. But as you probably know, nothing good in life ever comes that easily, so if you're ready for the long, hard slog, then go for it.

There are, of course, the stories of hugely successful writers like JK Rowling and Stephen King who collected seemingly endless rejection letters before they hit the big time, so I'm not saying give up if you want to go down the traditional publishing route – I'm just saying: be prepared. Research the industry and know what you're getting yourself into. Don't expect things to happen instantly, and don't be sad or disheartened if it takes a long time – this is normal. The more you know what to expect, the more positive you're likely to stay throughout the whole process, so don't get disheartened; get knowledgeable.

Many people decide to try and get a publishing deal while using the idea of self-publishing as a backup, but after years of trying and failing to get a publishing house interested, they realise they could have been using those years and all that wasted effort to write – and publish, and sell – more books. It's a hard choice, and one you'll have to make going on what your book is and how likely you think it's going to sell.

There are no rules about publishing and self-publishing when it comes to exclusivity, by the way – there have been quite a few success stories about writers who started out self-publishing and then got picked up by a major publisher when they became aware of how many books the authors were selling. Examples of this include Amanda Hocking, Hugh Howey, and Nick Spalding, if you want to look up their stories for inspiration. So that's another option: self-publish, and if you do well, use your already established platform and fan base to then approach publishers with. You never know.

Hybrid Publishing

For me personally, I love the idea of self-publishing, but if you really believe you have a brilliant book with huge marketing potential, then go for it, and don't take no for an answer! Many writers these days do both – they have deals for some of their books with traditional publishers (whether for ebooks or print books or both), and then they self-publish other titles, such as their back catalogue, or books that were previously published, the rights of which have reverted back to them. Some choose to approach traditional publishers with their more relevant, marketable work and then turn to self-publishing for titles that may not be so easy to market, or if their genre isn't so easy to distinguish. This is called hybrid publishing – doing a bit of both – and it is becoming more and more popular these days. If you're writing for yourself (what you like) rather than trying to write to a specific popular genre, then you may get more readers with self-publishing, where genres can be a little more fluid. If your book is more mainstream and marketable, it may have more luck with a traditional publisher. It really depends on what you're writing and how you want to distribute that writing.

I have nothing against traditional publishing (although I

am aware of how the industry is changing), and I would be very open to a traditional publishing deal if it happened to come my way, but I would definitely check the offer against what could be accomplished with self-publishing before I signed anything, and I'd definitely check the terms and conditions with regards to rights – movie rights, foreign publishing rights, and so on. If you're ever in this position, don't just blindly sign anything because of your excitement at getting a traditional publisher on board – go through the contract methodically and see how it compares to what you could achieve on your own.

There are plenty of great books out there on traditional vs. self-publishing, including the percentages you can make from each and how many books you'd have to sell to reach the same amount of profit. It's quite an eye-opener, and yet another argument for self-publishing growing in the future. For example, advances these days for traditionally-published writers might be less than you'd think, and you can often earn more by self-publishing a title and doing the marketing yourself, especially as self-publishing means that your book never goes out of print, compared to the limited print runs a traditional publisher may do, pulling your books from the shelves if they don't immediately sell as many copies as was first estimated.

Whatever you decide, make sure you've done the research first, and find a path that is best for you. If you'd like to find out more about self-publishing (or 'indie' publishing), then read ahead...

Self-Publishing

In case you hadn't already guessed, I'm a huge fan of self-publishing. Like many writers, I'm a bit of a control freak when it comes to my work, so the single biggest advantage (in my mind) of self-publishing is that you are in control of everything. If you wanted to, you could self-publish a ten page book on space squirrels with an awful cover and truly questionable writing skills and still have it sitting on Amazon waiting to be bought a few days later (although I wouldn't recommend this – you're not likely to get very good reviews or many sales!). You don't have to hit certain requirements, or write in a genre that's currently popular, or write something that is easily definable and easily marketable (although, of course, that helps). You get to choose the title and the cover of the book, and no one can tell you to change them at the last minute. You can end the book the way you want to end it, not in a way that would appeal to the biggest group of readers. You can write a standalone book or a series, and you can publish as many titles as you wish whenever you wish to publish them. Quite simply, there aren't really any rules, and for creative people, that is so refreshing and so exciting.

Self-publishing isn't new either. Take Beatrix Potter, for example. She was so tired of getting rejection letter after rejection letter for her book, *The Tale Of Peter Rabbit*, that she took matters into her own hands and organised the printing of the books herself. They were successful enough that she ended up getting picked up by one of the publishers she'd been rejected by, and this – in its basic form – shows the power of self-publishing, and the opportunities that can result from it.

Basically put, with self-publishing, you are in control. You write your book, you pay someone to proofread it or edit it if you can afford it, you get someone to design a cover (or find a premade one online, or design one yourself if you have the skills – I definitely don't), you make sure it's in the right format (again, you can pay someone to do this if you don't have the time or the patience to learn), and you then upload it to a website, or several websites. You can make them into ebooks, you can make them into paperbacks, or do a mix of both. My books are available as physical paperbacks, as ebooks for the Kindle, as ebooks for the Nook (Barnes and Noble), as ebooks on the Apple Store, and more. You pay nothing to upload them, then once the files have been reviewed and accepted, they're available to buy online (this may take a day or two, but what's a day or two compared to the amount of time it's taken you to get to this point)? Then, voila! Your book is for sale, and real people can buy it. It's quite impressive really.

Let's take a look at some aspects of self-publishing in a bit more depth, as these books are mostly aimed at self-publishing writers, and because if you're new to writing, you may not know as much about self-publishing as you do about publishing in the traditional sense. A lot has changed over the years, and you may find that your ideas about self-publishing are a little out-dated (I know mine were when I first started). Here are some things worth taking into account:

Saving Money: Years ago, self-publishing was seen as a last-resort for writers who couldn't get a traditional publishing deal. It was seen as difficult, expensive, and generally a major faff, which is why a lot of poor old manuscripts have never seen the light of day – a scary thought for a writer. I am very lucky to have started writing at a time when self-publishing was really coming into its own, and while I'm sure it will continue to change and improve over the next few years, I'm glad I came into it when I did. One of the main improvements in self-publishing over the last few years is that you don't have to spend all of your savings just to get your book published.

Gone are the days when you have to fork out thousands of pounds getting a hardback print run done of your book, leaving you with hundreds of books and nowhere to put them. Writers up and down the country filled their garages, their sheds, their spare rooms, the cupboards under their stairs and the spaces under their beds with their books, waiting for a time when they'd be able to sell all of them – a time which, for many, never came. They didn't have easy access to the Internet to do marketing, and they couldn't use Facebook or Twitter to build up an author platform. They would probably sell a few copies to friends and family members and then have to chuck the rest away, or leave the books to completely take over their house (and probably the houses of their friends and family members too). Some people still choose to do this today, which I don't really understand, but each to their own.

These days, we have this miraculous thing called Print On Demand (or POD), where we can upload our manuscripts and our covers, and order our books in much smaller quantities (or not at all, if selling primarily online through Amazon or other online bookstores). It's quick and it's easy, with minimum faff, but the best thing about this? There are no upfront costs. I repeat – there are no upfront costs! Sure, you might have shelled out some money to get the book proofread and formatted, and perhaps you spent a bit on the book cover, but this is small fry compared to what you could have been paying for a print run of hardbacks.

With Print On Demand sites such as Createspace, Lightning Source and IngramSpark (and there are more details on Createspace in particular in the next section), you simply set your price – as long as it's above the minimum to cover the costs of printing – and the website will simply pay you a percentage of the sale cost. Now, by looking at the percentage, some of you may think it's not much, but compared to what you could be earning with a traditional deal, it's actually pretty good, especially when you consider that the POD book can be up for sale forever, compared to traditional publishers who could pull your book from the shelves (virtual or otherwise) at any time. So money is a major factor, and it's probably the biggest thing that puts people off self-publishing, as they're still stuck with the idea of paying for print runs and having to house the physical copies themselves. Which brings me onto...

Saving Storage and Time: Self-publishing no longer relies on you storing your books yourself. In fact, as the 'demand' in Print On Demand suggests, they don't even get printed until someone orders one of your books. For example, I have my books available on Amazon, printed by their sister site, Createspace. I can order copies directly from Createspace when I need them, but as these come from America, there is an added shipping charge, a cost that changes depending on how soon you want your books to be delivered. Because of this, if I'm just ordering one copy, I'll usually go to Amazon and buy it as any other customer would, and as I have Amazon Prime (a yearly subscription fee you can pay to get free delivery, access to Prime Instant Video and more), it will be delivered to me – for free – the very next day. This saves me time, compared to the old model of self-publishing where you'd have to package and post each book yourself every time someone ordered one from you, and it also saves me space, as at no point do I have to come into contact with the book, and at no point do I have to store it in my house. A customer simply orders it from Amazon, Createspace prints the book and sends it out, and that's that. No further input (and therefore, no further time) is needed from me.

It's also worth comparing POD to traditional publishing, where they do have to order a print run of books, and they do have to store them in a warehouse somewhere until the bookstores have space on their shelves for them. If the book then doesn't sell at that bookstore, they can send the extra books back, something which the publisher may not have room for in their warehouse anymore. Guess what happens then? Well, it's not usually a happy ending – let's just put it that way.

<u>Saving The Hassle:</u> This is another reason why people get put off the idea of self-publishing, as they expect it to be this monumental nightmare that will eat up all of their time and leave them pulling their hair out. I won't lie: some parts can take a bit of getting used to, and it can take a while when you're starting out to get to grips with certain things, but that's all part of the fun! Once you've learnt the basics, however, it isn't hard to do them again, and each time you self-publish a book, you'll find that it gets quicker and easier as you realise that, actually, you *do* know what you're doing.

This, of course, can give you almost as much

satisfaction as receiving your finished book can, as you know that *you* did this, *you* made it all happen, and no one else. Some people also assume that there is zero hassle in traditional publishing as other people handle everything for you, and while in some respects that's correct, it doesn't mean that it's completely hassle-free. You still have to do the work of changing the manuscript if they don't like something, and you still have to interact with several different people while your book is going through the traditional publishing process. There can be delays, rewrites, things not going your way, and hundreds of other things that can make you want to tear your hair out. And even after the book's published, it isn't guaranteed that the hassle will stop – these days, authors are expected to take part in their own marketing even if they're with a traditional publisher, and most authors put a lot of time and effort into this in an attempt to stop their book from being dropped from the shelves a few months down the line. This doesn't exactly sound hassle-free to me, so you'll have to decide for yourself which kind of hassle you're more likely to put up with.

Personally, I don't think of self-publishing tasks as being a hassle – I think of them as learning experiences for my future books, and I take what I can from any problems I come across. The more I learn, the easier I know it'll be to do my next book, so I try not to scream when something takes a little longer than I expected it to. Plus, with self-publishing, you're usually working to your own timescale, which takes a lot of the stress away from getting your book ready. The only person you have to please – initially – is you. Then, the readers, of course, but initially, just you.

<u>Saving Years Of Your Life:</u> Yes, some people think of self-publishing as being very time-consuming, and that they'd rather spend the time pursuing a traditional publishing deal, but when you think about it, self-publishing can save you a hell of a lot of time in the long-run. Authors who see traditional publishing as some sort of status symbol, or who don't understand how self-publishing works these days, can literally spend years of their lives chasing after that perfect traditional publishing contract (which may or may not exist for them), and while some of these writers will undoubtedly get somewhere with their books, others will not, meaning that years and years have come to nothing.

If you self-publish, your work is available instantly – let me repeat that: your work is available instantly! OK, so it might take a day or so to be available, but one day versus years of your life? I know which one I'd rather choose. Yes, there is then the time you need to spend building your author platform and marketing your book, but as I've mentioned, you'd probably have to do that anyway if you had a traditional contract, and you'll hopefully be seeing sales coming in while you're doing all that stuff, which will most definitely make it completely worthwhile. Just think – if you have a great book or books, and if you have some decent marketing going on – you could sell thousands of copies in those few years compared to selling none while going after that elusive contract. It's worth thinking about, at any rate.

I truly believe that self-publishing is the way forward (although I realise it won't be for everyone) and so far I've loved the experience of publishing my own books. I plan to do it for a long time to come, and the more I read about it and the more I learn, the easier I find it to do. There is definitely still a stigma attached to indie publishing – some writers will always think of it as being 'the easy way out', not giving self-published writers the attention and respect they deserve, and thinking of it as somehow being less important than being traditionally published. But the time is coming when those writers – and readers – will have to start changing their tune. The industry is constantly evolving as e-readers, tablets, phones and other technology all improve, and impressions of self-publishing are changing too. It is no longer thought to be the last resort of writers who can't write, and it is coming into its own as something writers can do to get their work out there and actually make some money.

As self-publishing is changing and improving all the time, it can be a little hard to keep up with everything, but if you do, I promise you a fun and rewarding experience, and seeing your own books on your own bookshelf is one of the best feelings a writer can have. Plus, the traditional publishing industry is changing all the time, and keeping up with that can be similar to trying to keep up with the self-publishing industry, so it really is worth doing your homework and figuring out which route is the best for you. Only you can know that, and as they say, knowledge is power. Go forth and gain knowledge! Then decide on traditional vs. self-publishing.

I think what you have to do is make sure that you're aware of traditional publishing, self-publishing, and the pros and cons of both. Don't think of getting your book published in the same way you might have had to fifty, thirty, or even ten years ago. The industry is constantly changing (have I said that already?), and with it now being easier than ever to publish and sell your own books, it is definitely worth looking into. If you're a bit of a book snob and turn your nose up at things like ebooks and e-readers, then you probably need to start changing your attitude – as with most things in life, books are evolving, and if you don't evolve with them, you'll be left behind. Plus, ebooks save trees, so how can that be a bad thing?

There are countless websites on traditional publishing vs. self-publishing, so many in fact that it can be rather overwhelming, so I recommend stepping back from your computer for a while and reading an actual book (let's ignore the tree thing for a few minutes!). The *Writers' & Artists' Yearbook* is pretty much the bible of publishing in the UK, whether you want to self-publish or go down the traditional route. It has a hell of a lot of info in, including interviews with well known writers, and lists of publishers, agents and other useful people to contact if you want to try it the traditional way. This great resource gets updated every year, and the 2012 *Writers' & Artists' Yearbook* actually convinced me to try self-publishing, after reading the book through from front to back and calculating how long it would likely take me to get a traditional publisher on board – if, indeed, if ever happened. That was my reaction to the book, but you may well have the opposite reaction. Whatever the book convinces you to do, it will convince you to do something, and therefore it is a great inspirational tool. You can get this book from the Writers & Artists website (www.writersandartists.co.uk – also a very useful site), for around £20, and there's also a *Children's Writers' & Artists'* Yearbook if you're into writing books for kids.

If you'd rather get your information for free online, however, there are several websites that will fill your head with all sorts of information regarding traditional, self, and hybrid publishing. Here are just a few, and they are also listed in the Resources section in the appendix:

The Write Life Self-Publishing vs. Traditional Infographic - thewritelife.com/se
Scribendi Traditional Publishing vs. Self-publishing - www.scribendi.com/advice/traditional_versus_self_publ ishing.en.html
Miami Herald 'Self-publishing vs. traditional publishing: How to choose?' - www.miamiherald.com/news/business/biz-monday/article3950085.html
Jane Friedman – Self-Publish or Perish - janefriedman.com/leap-to-indie/
The Guardian 'Traditional publishing is 'no longer fair or sustainable', says Society of Authors - www.theguardian.com/books/2014/jul/11/traditional-publishing-fair-sustainable-society-of-authors
Self-Publish Or Not - http://www.underdown.org/self-publish.htm
Nielsen: Self-Publishing Now More Like Traditional Publishing - publishingperspectives.com/2015/06/nielsen-self-publishing-now-more-like-traditional-publishing/

Vanity Publishing

I'd like to briefly make a note of vanity publishers here. In my day job of running Coleman Editing (a proofreading, editing and ghostwriting service), I see a lot of people who contact me after they've completed their manuscript, overjoyed that they've just got off the phone with a publisher who's interested in publishing their work. I enthuse with them – getting published in any way is great news, as it gets your book out there – but more often than not, my clients are referring to vanity publishers, without really realising what they are and what it means to be published with them.

First of all, a real publisher would never charge you to publish your book – why would they? You're the one who's done the work, and they're the people who stand to make money out of you if your book is a success. If you're paying someone to publish your book, they're more than likely a vanity publisher. Secondly, vanity publishers make a hell of a lot of money from writers who go to them, so they say yes to everyone. If you've been accepted by a vanity publisher, it doesn't mean they like your work. They won't have even read it (apart from maybe a few companies who operate differently – I am generalising here, but more than likely, this is what they're doing). So many clients tell me they can't believe they've been accepted by a publisher (and that they read their manuscript so quickly), when really it's just a vanity publisher saying 'yes' to everyone and everything because it will make them more money, no matter what – if they're getting thousands per author, they're making a whole heap of money for not really doing that much.

Basically, vanity publishers are companies who charge you to publish your own book. And by publish, it usually means have them printed in a short print run that you can then sell yourself. They'll probably list the title on their website, and have it available to buy directly from them as well, but that's as much as you're likely to get in terms of marketing help, and you'll soon realise that you've shelled out hundreds if not thousands of pounds just to get your book printed – something you can do yourself with Print On Demand services like Createspace. Your book will be available online, yes, and if that's what you're aiming for and you're willing to pay someone else to do it, that's fine, but if you're willing to put in a little extra time (and what's a bit of time compared to how long you've been writing your novel for?), then you can learn how to do the basics yourself, using sites such as Createspace and Amazon to make your dreams a reality.

I'm not talking about printers here, by the way. Some people (who only want so many copies to sell themselves and aren't interested in being online at all) may just want to get a short print run of their books, so they'll find a printer who can do it for a certain price. This isn't what I mean by vanity publishing. These publishers will call themselves publishers rather than printers, and they'll offer you a 'publishing package' in exchange for hundreds or thousands of your well-earned pounds. Some may offer more in their package, such as proofreading, editing and formatting – in which case, fair enough – but if they're just going to print the book for you and list it on their website, it's really not going to be worth it.

Amazon and Createspace

Again, I'm not going to go into great detail about how you can self-publish, as there are loads of books out there on the subject already (not to mention some brilliantly useful websites), but I want to at least touch on it here if you're just starting out and are unfamiliar with the options. I think that a lot of the time, people are put off the idea of self-publishing because they have preconceived notions of what it entails: they think it means paying a lot of money up front, something you don't need to do (and shouldn't be doing, so you might want to rethink that vanity publisher if you're shelling out huge amounts of money), and they think that it involves a lot of skill.

The truth is, anything you don't know how to do, you can either learn how to do it yourself or you can hire someone to do it for you, and it doesn't have to cost you the earth. The main things you need are someone to format the book (you can do this yourself by reading website tutorials or downloading ebooks that will take you through it step by step), and someone to design you a cover. I mention book cover designers in another section, but you can get a premade cover for as little as £30, so it doesn't have to break the bank.

Proofreading and editing your book is likely to be the biggest cost to your self-publishing venture, and while it's highly recommended not to skip this step, if you don't have the money, at least get some people to beta read your book for you (perhaps in exchange for a paperback copy of the book once it's released), and if you have any friends or family members who are reading fans, ask them (very nicely) if they can proofread it for you. Just make sure you make it very clear that you want them to be ruthless, you don't want them to be nice, and that them turning round and saying 'it's very good' will be no help whatsoever. Whatever you do, get a second (and possibly third and fourth) pair of eyes on your manuscript before you publish it.

You may have gone over it a million times yourself, but this in itself can be a problem – if you've read the same thing over and over again (knowing what you meant to write), you may miss that typo; your eye will just travel straight over it because your brain will be filling in the gaps as you go, knowing what it is you've been writing about and knowing what that sentence is *supposed* to say, even if it doesn't actually say it. A lot of traditionally published books still have the occasional typo, so it's nothing to be too concerned about if one tiny thing slips through the net, but it is worth getting a 'fresh' pair of eyes to read through it before you publish.

After this, you don't need to pay any money up front in order to self-publish your work, and neither should you. If you're just starting out with self-publishing, the easiest way of getting your book out there in the two most popular formats are by uploading it to Amazon Kindle Direct Publishing – this will give you an ebook that people can download onto their Kindles or Kindle apps – and Createspace, Amazon's sister site that make Print On Demand paperbacks. It's brilliant – I love it (and no, they're not paying me to say that!). The dream of holding a physical copy of your book in your hands is just days away; once you've uploaded the manuscript and the cover, and once Createspace have checked the files, it can be ready in the Createspace store – and on Amazon – within a couple of days. The same with KDP – you just need to upload your manuscript and cover, write your product description, get it all checked over, and voila! You have an ebook ready to buy from Amazon. People will actually be able to go onto

Amazon, search for your name, and have it pop up –
like a 'real' author (which, of course, you now are)!

Even just a few years ago, this wasn't possible, so make
the most of the technology that is available to you now.
You don't have to pay up front for hundreds of
hardback copies, and you don't have to find somewhere
in your house to store them all until you sell them. Print
On Demand is exactly that – even if just one person
orders just one copy of your book, Createspace will
print it and ship it off to them without you having to lift
a finger (and if your customer is a member of Amazon
Prime, they'll often get it the very next day for no extra
charge – now that's service). You don't pay a penny up
front, and you get a percentage of the sale every time
someone purchases a copy (up to 70% of the sale price
with ebooks). That's often more than you'd get per copy
compared to if you'd gone down the traditional route,
and it'll be available a hell of a lot quicker as well.

Just a quick word about ISBNs here – these are the
numbers you find on books that allow them to be
catalogued in stores, and it can be a bit tricky to get
your head around it all. If you're self-publishing and
you want the freedom to try and sell your books in
stores and so on, it's advisable to pay for your own
ISBN numbers (available in sets of 10 from Nielsen in
the UK). Luckily, there are some easy ways of dealing
with them and getting them for free. For example,
Createspace gives you the option to get a free one from
them, but this will only be for the Createspace version
of the paperback, and the same with Smashwords: you
can get a free Smashwords ISBN so that your ebooks
can be added to the Premium catalogue and sent out to
other online stores, but 'Smashwords' will be noted as

the publisher for that particular ebook. It's worth reading up on, and while it may seem a little confusing, you'll soon get used to it all.

Smashwords

As someone who loves Amazon and Createspace when it comes to self-publishing my own books, I've only recently started using Smashwords as another way of getting my books out there, and honestly, I wish I'd done it sooner. The site is just so easy to use, and your books look great once you've uploaded them (and listed them as a series if applicable). If you haven't used it before, it's basically just a great site to find ebooks (both free and paid) in all genres and in both fiction and non-fiction. You can download them in several different files depending on how you want to read them, and you can add books to your reader libraries for the future. Check it out as a reader first to get used to it.

When it comes to self-publishing on Smashwords, I found the whole process of uploading and listing books to be incredibly easy, and the dashboard is great, giving you an ISBN manager (you can get free ISBNs for your Smashwords ebooks), pricing manager, VAT manager, and series manager if you have books that form a series. It has an easy layout, and it's easy to organise your books how you want them – it's just easy in general. You can also do some pretty useful stuff with Smashwords like giving coupons to people for your books, and you can list your book as being permanently free, something that Amazon doesn't allow unless your books are free and available elsewhere on the net. Smashwords also allows you to answer an online interview about yourself and your writing for prospective readers to have a look at, and there's lots of other fun stuff as well. If your book files match their requirements, you can also get 'Premium Status', which means that your ebooks will be listed on the Barnes and Noble website (for the Nook e-reader) and on the Apple iBooks store. This is done without any further input from you, and it only takes a few days to be approved, so that's pretty great.

The only thing I would say about Smashwords is that in order to distribute your manuscript in as many formats as possible, they have a strict format/layout that you need to submit your work in. They offer a free style guide to help, but it's long and complicated, and you can get someone (recommended by Smashwords) to do the formatting for you for around £30 – £60 depending on the length of your manuscript. This saves a lot of time and also saves the bashing of your head against the keyboard, so I think it's worth it. If you then upload your perfectly formatted word document, Smashwords will transform it (within a couple of minutes and quite magically) into several different formats, ready to be purchased and downloaded: epub, mobi (Kindle), pdf, and more. It really is rather clever, so why not check it out?

Here are a few links to the sites I've mentioned above, and these are also listed in the Resources section of the appendix:

<u>Amazon Kindle Direct Publishing</u> - kdp.amazon.com
<u>Createspace</u> - www.createspace.com
<u>Lightning Source</u> - www.lightningsource.com
<u>IngramSpark</u> - www.ingramspark.com
<u>Smashwords</u> - www.smashwords.com

Nielsen (UK ISBN Agency) -
www.isbn.nielsenbook.co.uk/controller.php?page=121
Writers & Artists - www.writersandartists.co.uk

Now that we've sorted out our self-doubt problems and gone over the publishing options a little bit, it's time to get serious, and by serious, I mean fun. Are you ready to get into that creative writing headspace? Are you ready to start writing? Are you ready to get creating? Then let's go!

Plotting And Planning

Some writers can sit down at their computers and just write, but most of us have to do at least some planning and plotting before we start. I know I do – for my Little Forest series of books, I now do a 20,000 word plan before I even start writing, so I know exactly what happens in each scene, which speeds up the actual writing process no end. Of course, different people work differently, and you may work better from a simple outline (with freedom to deviate from it) than you do from a detailed, structured plan.

In general, plotting and planning can sound like a bit of a chore, but it doesn't have to be boring, and the more you plan your book, the easier it should be when you do come to sit down and write it.

Scrivener

I mention Scrivener elsewhere in these books, but as well as writing the book and getting the layout done at the end, Scrivener's corkboard feature can be a great (and fun) way to plan your storyline. Plus, it's a hell of a lot less messy than covering your entire house in actual post-its (although, that's also an option – maybe don't do it at work, though).

Yes, the corkboard mode is – in my opinion – the main thing that makes Scrivener great for planning your novel. You can split your book into chapters (or parts and then chapters), and then you can split your chapters into scenes. When using the corkboard view, you can then move these scenes around if you decide you don't like the order, and it's so easy to add bits in and take bits out if you're not sure about certain elements of your book. The more you play around with it, the easier you'll find it (and the more features you'll discover). You can read more about Scrivener in the 'Ways To Write' section.

Excel Spreadsheet

Another one from good old Microsoft Office, I often use Excel to create spreadsheets for my writing. I love spreadsheets. I have them for my business (keeping track of my clients, my work, my invoices, my incomings, my expenses, everything), but I also have them for my own projects. I have one spreadsheet, for example, detailing all of the project ideas I've ever had, from short stories to standalone novels, screenplays to series. They're all nicely colour coded (you've got to love colour coding) and ready and waiting for when I have the time to write them. I find that colour coding can stop anything from being boring, but maybe that's just me. My spreadsheet is quite old now, so if you decide to do this for yourself, just make sure you always have a copy backed up. Every time I update it I usually email it to myself as well, just as an extra precaution – I wouldn't be able to remember all the ideas on my own, and you never know when one might come in useful.

Evernote

I just thought I'd put a little bit in here about this app as it can be quite useful when starting to think about that novel or story you're going to write. It's basically a quick and easy way of taking note of things you see that could be useful to your story planning. You can write (both short notes and longer pieces), you can collect images and pictures that inspire you, and a lot more. It's a sort of fun organiser, and you can put it on your tablet and phone for when you're out and about and you see something really inspirational. You can get the 'basic' app for free.

Presenting Your Book – 'Plan How You Know'

We've all heard of writing what you know, so why don't we take this idea when it comes to planning our stories? If you don't often use word processing in your daily life, planning something using Word may not come easily to you at all. The same with Excel – I love creating spreadsheets (spreadsheet nerd alert) as I use them anyway when running my business, but to people who don't use them, the idea of starting one in order to plan your story can be a bit of a nightmare. So, why not take what you do in your daily life and apply that to your planning?

Do you work for a company where you often have to do presentations to clients and/or other colleagues? Do you use programs like PowerPoint or Keynote in order to do this? Do you know the software inside out and could come up with a presentation in your sleep? If so, why not use it to plan your novels? Using programs we have experience with and that we feel comfortable with can really help when we're planning our work, as our brains don't have to deal with learning all the technical stuff, allowing them to really get into all the creative stuff instead.

If you're going to make a PowerPoint/Keynote style presentation, why not do what you'd do with a meeting and try and get the main points of each scene into just one slide? Or have a slide per character, using bullet points to describe their main personality traits and information regarding their work life, social life, and personal life. You can even add a drawing you've done of the character or put in an image you found online that resembles the image you have of them in your head. Create a slide for themes, and one for listing secondary characters. Have a slide for each main location, describing the place and how it's used within the novel. Really have some fun with it.

Once you've got your finished presentation, you can use it in a few different ways. You can show it to family and friends and see what they think about your initial ideas, getting feedback for when you actually come to write your book, and you can also use it during the writing process when you need a little inspiration or a reminder of what you should be writing!

Non-computer Planning

I mentioned post-its all over the house, but going along this line of thought doesn't have to be completely ridiculous. If you're lucky enough to have a home office, use a corkboard or fashion something on one wall to use as your novel planner, sticking up post-its and bits of paper that you can move around when you switch your scenes. If you want to go all out, use pictures and images as well to really help visualise the story, locations and characters, linking them with lines or bits of string for that TV detective feel.

Yes, it may sound stupid, but making the planning stage fun will really help – it will make you want to carry on and get that story written, instead of drowning in a sea of boring word processor documents. Just don't go too far down the detective route – otherwise, you might find that your friends and family stop talking to you. Obviously, this method is far more useful (and satisfying) if you're plotting out a crime novel or whodunit, and you might even find it so fun that before you know it, you've plotted out an entire series of books. Well, you never know; it *could* happen.

Planning Big

We've mentioned a notepad and pen, but one thing I found useful when planning the first five books of my Little Forest series was using a giant notepad (and I mean huge – it was a large sketching pad meant for artists, which when standing up, was pretty much like a flipboard). I got a variety of coloured markers, and I went to town. I used this to plan my novels, and to add in the main points of each as I went along, so I could refer back to them when I was writing the next book in the series. There's something about the size that made it easy to use – I use notepads a lot (for a lot of different projects) so this was something different, and by using such a large book to write my notes in, it made me think of the project in a different way too: this was my main project, the one that took up most space in my room and my mind. It can also be a good way of mind mapping, and of scribbling and doodling when you're trying to plan your plots and storylines.

World Building

If you're writing a fiction book based in a fictional place, you're probably going to have to do some world building. This can be fun – really fun, if you do it right – but what if you're setting your story in a real place, but one you've never visited? Or somewhere you visited once, got swept off your feet by, and simply had to set your novel there, but with no idea about the particular geography of the place? If you've got the money, you can visit that place – and if you're really serious about being a writer, you can justify it to yourself as an investment in your future – but of course this isn't feasible to most of us. So do the next best thing: research. This can be almost as much fun, and you have the added bonus of being able to do it in bed in your pyjamas with a nice cup of tea if you want to.

The old-fashioned way to do this would be to order a load of guide books and maps of your chosen location, and some people may still prefer to do this – pin the map up on a pin board and mark out the main locations where things 'go down' in your story. This red pin is where the murder victim was found, that gold sticker is where the two main characters kissed for the first time… you get the idea. You can even come up with some kind of elaborate code so the scenes are noted as to their chronological order too, but I imagine most people wouldn't have the time (or the desire) to do this!

This technique (which is also mentioned elsewhere in these books as a way of planning your novel) would work particularly well if you're writing a crime story, or a series based on a detective – just the act of pinning up maps, images, and notes could help you get into the detective mindset, you never know. Just make sure you don't start covering every wall of your house with pictures and scribbles – your family probably won't thank you for it, and you might have to sit through an intervention from your well-meaning friends.

The more modern way of scoping out a place is, of course, to use the Internet. Check out Google Maps for your scene setting, and then switch to satellite view or street view for a different perspective – street view is particularly useful for getting a feel of a city or place you've never visited. Then there's Google Earth and other sites/apps that can let you explore a location from the comfort of your own home. Use estate agent sites and rental searches to get a feel of the properties in a said town or city, and even hotels and B&B finder sites can help get a feel for a place. For example, check out the places available on Air B&B – you'll not only get a sense of the types of houses people live in, but also the types of people who live there.

Of course, if you're creating a fictional location for your story, all of these things still apply; you can just use the sites and apps as inspiration instead of solid research. Want a city like London but with its own fictional quirks? Take some aspects of the real London and then shape the rest of the city how you want it to be. After all, in your own story, there are no right or wrong answers – it's all up to you.

World building for your novel or series of novels can be a long and complicated task, but it can also be really fun. How often do you get to create entire worlds? You can choose what your city or town or village is like, you can choose who lives where, where your main characters hang out, and a million other little details that will really make your book come to life. For sci-fi and fantasy genres, you can pretty much do whatever you want in the world you're creating, turning everything upside down if you wish to. What I'm going to focus on in this section is simpler – this is for if your story is based mainly in the 'real' world, but you need to create believable people and places to populate your novel with.

Here are just a few ideas and questions to get you thinking about your own world, from the locations to the characters and other bits and bobs it can be worth planning before you start writing your novel.

Locations

I created several locations for my Little Forest series of novels, mainly:

Little Forest – the village where most of the main characters live and where most of the action takes place, at least in the first book, *The Former World*.
Renfield – the next village along, the gang start spending more time here from *Memento Mori* onwards.

Durwich – the third of the three villages in their cluster, Beth starts attending group meetings here in *Carnival Masquerade*.

Upper Runville – a smaller village than Little Forest that Beth discovers she has a strong link to.

Willowton – the nearest town, with more shops and opportunities in terms of work.

Birston – the nearest big city, where Beth and her friends go for proper shopping trips and visits to the theatre.

Ballycave – the village in Ireland that Connor and the gang visit in *The Gloaming*.

Covershire – this is the county which covers all of the above cities, towns and villages.

Once you start designing one fictional place, you'll no doubt find that you need to keep on creating more and more, especially if you're writing a series and need to keep things fresh and interesting by having your characters visit new towns and cities. If you have one main location, however, it's worth spending more time on that than anything else. I spent a long time thinking about the layout of Little Forest for the first novel, but I also thought ahead about how I'd need to use the village in the upcoming books, especially with characters moving house and making friends with new characters in different villages. I also drew a rather detailed map for Little Forest village that I referred back to when writing *The Former World*.

Here are some location questions to get you thinking. Let's start with the simple stuff:

What is the name of your location?
What is the type of setting (village/town/city/other)?

What country is it set in?

Whereabouts (roughly) in the country is the location supposed to be? E.g. Is it landlocked or by the coast?

What is the rough population?

Are all of your locations fictional or will you be using/referring to real places too?

Where does your main character live?

Where do your secondary characters live in relation to your main character?

How would you describe the place in basic terms – rural/urban? Posh/rough? Desirable/cheap to live in?

How would you describe the location if it were on a postcard?

What is the terrain like?

Are there any tourist attractions, and if so, what are they?

Are there any pubs/bars/clubs, and if so, what are they?

Are there any restaurants, and if so, what are they?

Are there any town hall type places? Any councils or government buildings?

Are there any libraries/theatres?

Are there any historical sites – castles, stately homes, or similar places of interest?

Are there police stations/fire stations/hospitals/doctors?

What kinds of shops and services are available there?

Is there a prison?

What fun things are there to do there?

Is there any countryside/are there places to walk around the area?

Are there lakes, rivers, or other bodies of water?

OK, now let's get down to the nitty gritty (this will depend heavily on your chosen genre, but as an example, I'm thinking of crime/murder mystery type books):

Are there any dark secrets in your location's past?

Have there been any murders in the area? If so, what are the details and when did they occur?

Who runs the location? Local council, local members of parliament, mayor, police?

Who runs it unofficially? Is there a rich businessman who oversees the place? Are there any illegal gangs or people with dodgy connections pulling the strings?

Describe your character's house – the number of rooms, the layout, the exterior, the garden. Is it a council house? Is it an old building? Is it an expensive new build with all the best quality furnishings? What does it say about your character (and their family, if necessary)?

Are the other houses in the area similar or do they differ? Describe a few different houses.

Describe the main population in terms of age, social class, race, and so on.

Describe the location in great detail (and/or draw a map). Include road names, locations of houses and businesses, pathways that your main character usually takes, where they work, and other places of interest. Make sure they all work together for the purposes of your plot, and if you're planning a series, think ahead to what else you need to include in the area.

If you're writing sci-fi or fantasy, the questions you need to ask yourself will obviously be different to these, and they'll probably go deeper into the hierarchy of your characters, how the place is run and by whom, and the general government/ruling party and how things work on a daily basis. If you're setting your novel in the normal world, it will be more basic, but don't make the mistake of keeping it *too* basic; your readers need to feel that this place – this world – exists, and the settings you use are just as important as your characters and your story.

Characters

Creating characters for your novel can be fun, but it can be harder than you think, especially once you've got past your protagonist, your antagonist, and your other main characters. As you get into the minor characters, how do you make sure they're different enough from each other? How can you make sure your readers won't get confused? How can you make sure that you, the writer, won't get confused?

It's a simple thing, but I find that creating a thorough character profile for each person – no matter how minor or how little they are involved in the plot – can really help. You can do this in a variety of ways, from typing it into Word, writing it in a notepad so you can have easy access to it when you're writing, or even using computer programs that give you space to write down character information (think Scrivener, for example). Some people also find it useful to add images to their character profiles, whether from drawings they've done themselves, people they've found on Google Images, or photos they've found on one of the stock photos site. You can even use images of celebrities for guidance, but this doesn't always work for everyone – once you've pictured Johnny Depp or Matt Damon in your lead role, you'll find it hard to picture anyone else.

So, what to put in the actual character profile? You can add in any amount of detail that you want, but I've come up with a few questions for you to answer so you can really get a feel for your character, and so you can understand their actions and motivations. It's not just about what they look like, or what job they do, or who they live with – you've really got to get to the bottom of the characters' pasts, feelings, and personalities. You've got to think of them as real people, because to your readers, they will be (well, hopefully, anyway!)

Here are some character profile questions to get you thinking. Let's start with the simple stuff:

Name?
DOB?
Relationship status?
Physical appearance?
Any scars or tattoos?
Style – what kind of clothes do they like wearing?
What is their job?
What qualifications do they have?
Where is their place of residence?
Who do they live with?
Who is in their close and extended family?
Who are their main friends?
Where did they go to school?
Main likes?
Main dislikes?
Do they own any pets?
Favourite band, TV show and film?

OK, now let's get down to the nitty gritty:

Have they ever been in love? If so, describe their partner and how they fell for each other.
What is their biggest regret in life?
What are their biggest fears?

What activities and places to visit are on their bucket list?

How would they react if they found themselves in a fight?

What would they say are their best features / personality traits?

What would they say are their worst features / personality traits?

What three celebrities – dead or alive – would they have at their fantasy dinner party?

What is their most secret desire?

What is their dream occupation?

Name something they've never told anyone about:

What is their most embarrassing moment?

What qualities do they most admire in the opposite sex?

What qualities do they look for in their friends?

How do they relate to their family members?

Describe a past event that had a big impact on their life:

What is their favourite quote (funny, inspirational, motivational etc.)?

Who do they most admire in the whole world and why?

What is the worst thing they've ever done in their life?

What is the craziest thing they've ever done in their life?

What are their goals and ambitions?

Well, you get the idea. You need to get inside your characters' heads, and make sure you know everything about them. Of course, you don't need to go into quite as much detail for the really minor characters, but just thinking about this will help you when you need to write a difficult scene, or when you don't know how they'd react under certain circumstances, or if you're not sure what they'd say when confronted by someone they didn't like. Just look at what you've written down about their personality and their past, and apply that to the scene. The more you do this, the easier it will become.

So, why not try filling in a character profile for your protagonist right now? It will help you with your book, and more than anything else, it can be a pretty fun task to do! Your characters will thank you for it.

Extras

My Little Forest series is set in the 'real' world, but with fictional towns and cities as well as paranormal elements. The characters mention real life places – such as Manchester, Edinburgh and London – but I also make use of a lot of fictional places in both England and Ireland. The characters are aware of real life pop culture and events, but they also have their own 'celebrities' in their own world – bands, entertainers, well known local businessmen and so on. You'll need to decide how much of the real world you want to allude to, and how much of your made up world your characters will be dealing with. For certain genres you may need to ignore the 'real' world completely, and for others you might come up with your own characters but use the places and events of the real world, without needing to make up a whole lot of stuff. Take a while to consider what extras you'll need to include in your world building.

You can find the World Building Cheat Sheets in the appendix for easy access.

Book Covers For Motivation

One of the most rewarding parts of writing, I find (and this is more in terms of self-publishing than traditional publishing), is when you've got the story all done and dusted and you're looking to sort out the cover. Whether you're buying a premade one, getting a designer to do a bespoke cover for you, or making one yourself, this is the moment when everything starts coming together. You can finally picture what your book will look like listed on the web or when you're handing out copies to your family, and you can look at that cover and know that you've achieved your first goal – completing that novel. It's a great feeling, but it's not one you necessarily have to wait for.

Even if you're thinking about going down the traditional publishing route (where, if you're successful, you'll be unlikely to have any input into what your cover looks like), this is still a great motivational exercise to do. And, at the very least, it will get you thinking about covers, genres, and your brand.

Premade Covers

First of all, have a look at several book cover designer

sites and see which style you like. Some websites are run by individuals, so their designs are all likely to have a similar, uniform style to them, while others feature covers from hundreds of different designers, so take a while to have a good look around. Then, browse through the covers while thinking about the story you want to write. It doesn't matter if you have the entire novel already planned out or if you only have an idea of a genre and a main character; if you see a cover that would fit your story perfectly, you'll know it.

Now, you can leave it there and just picture that cover every time you need a burst of inspiration, or you can go one step further. If you see a cover you love and that would fit your book anyway, it's a good idea to buy it right then and there, as it may not be available when you've finished your book. Purchasing that cover could be the difference between finishing your novel and giving up, especially if you start to lose track of why you're writing it in the first place.

Now, if you're going to buy a cover, the designer will ask you for the details: author name, title of book, subtitle etc. If you don't yet know what your book is going to be called, you can either decide on a title now (what's on the cover may give you some inspiration here), or you can ask the designer if you can pay now and get the details updated in a few months. At the very least you can come up with a temporary title for now and get it changed later (although you'll probably have to pay more money to get this done).

The idea is that you have a finished book cover (probably just an ebook cover for now as you won't know the dimensions of your paperback until after you've written it) that you can open on your computer and look at whenever you're starting to feel hopeless about the whole project (and there more than likely *will* be those moments, believe me!). Better yet, print out the cover and stick it on your wall next to your computer, or on your mirror so you'll see it when you wake up in the morning. I suppose it's the same thing that some people do when they want to lose weight – they stick a photo of them at their optimum weight on the front of the fridge, or a picture of someone whose figure they admire. It's all about motivation and having a constant reminder of what you're working towards, of what you want to achieve. Of course, this will only really work if you've got a kickass cover, so maybe don't use one of your own design if you have no experience of making graphics (it may even put you off)!

Stock Photos

Another way of doing this is by looking at photos or images instead of predesigned book covers. Head over to Google images and take a look around, or use stock photo sites and apps such as iStockphoto, Shutterstock, Fotolia and others. Just see what's available, and what kind of images you can imagine using on your cover (or covers if you're planning a series). These images might even give you more ideas, and you can start creating a virtual (or actual) scrapbook for inspiration – more of this in the 'Get Crafty' section.

There's more of this in the 'Design Your Own Cover' section, but if you do end up buying any stock photos, be aware of the licensing rules (also applicable if you purchase any fonts). If you go for just the basic standard license, there will be conditions you need to know about, the main one being that you can only use the image so many times. In Fotolia's case (just to give you an example), a standard license will not allow you to use the image more than 500,000 times. For most people, this will be fine, but if you're thinking big (and if you're not – why not?) it may be worth going for the extended license (sometimes called commercial license) where there's no limit on the amount of times you can use it.

It's worth reading through all the terms and conditions on stock photo websites (and font sites) just to make sure you know what you're getting into, and it's also worth noting that you don't actually own the image you buy – other people can buy it too (which is why you'll often see very similar book covers by authors who have just taken the stock image and done nothing to change it). You're essentially renting it, and just like when you're renting a house, there's nothing to stop the landlord/stock photo owner from 'evicting' you from its use. If they pull down the photo, you simply have to use another image – a bit annoying if you've successfully got sales from your amazing book cover, but there's not much you can do about it. It's just something to be aware of.

Here are some stock photo websites you can use to find that perfect image, also listed in the Resources section in the appendix:

Fotolia - en.fotolia.com
Shutterstock - www.shutterstock.com
iStock - www.istockphoto.com
Bigstock - www.bigstockphoto.com
Getty Images - www.gettyimages.co.uk

Premade book covers can vary in price – from around £15 to £80 – and obviously bespoke covers will cost much more, but even if you don't end up using the exact same cover when you come to self-publish (and even if you're sending your manuscript out to agents and publishers), I still think it's a great investment if it gives you that push you need to get your book finished (or started!). Just picture how good that book is going to look on your shelf, with its awesome shiny cover and your name in capitals across the front. Keep picturing the finished product until you get there!

By spending real money on it, you're also more likely to carry on using it as a motivational tool, instead of just forgetting about it. So, whenever you're feeling a lack of inspiration, you can open up that book cover and have a good old stare at it: this is what your book will look like when it's finished, and it looks awesome, so you'd better get writing! Plus, you spent money on it, so it would be a waste if you weren't to get that book finished.

I actually did this for the three books in this *Creative Ways to Start Creative Writing* series. I'd just found a new cover website that I hadn't seen before, and I was immediately drawn to it. The covers were very good, there was a wide range for different genres as well as non-fiction, and the humour of the guy who runs the site got me laughing – some of his fake book titles are hilarious. I found the cover I wanted, then I bought three of them, asking the designer (James at Goonwrite.com) to create two more covers from the first, but slightly tweaked to show they were different books in the same series. There was a financial reason for this (he offered a discount if you paid for more covers at a time) as well as a practical reason (I didn't want the cover to be sold before I'd finished the books) but I also did it for motivation.

I'd had the idea for this series of books for a while (I usually write fiction so it seemed like non-fiction would be a nice change), and because of how busy I am, I knew that if I didn't have a really good reason to write it, I'd just let it slide in favour of my full time business/day job and my upcoming novels. Spending money on not one but three new covers meant that I *had* to finish these books, and having the covers already on my computer – for me to look at whenever I wanted – helped me to visualise the finished projects, thinking how good it would feel to have all three of them up for sale, and – hopefully – helping other writers to get in the creative zone. I only bought the ebook covers first, however – I had to wait to get the Createspace cover done until I knew how long each book would be.

Some great cover designers are listed here and in the Resources section at the end of the book:

GoOnWrite - www.goonwrite.com
Creative Paramita - http://www.creativeparamita.com
The Book Cover Designer -
www.thebookcoverdesigner.com
The Cover Collection - www.thecovercollection.com
Tanya Back Designs - www.tanyaback.com
Ebook Indie Covers - ebookindiecovers.com
The Book Cover Machine -
bookcovermachine.wordpress.com
Spiffing Covers - www.spiffingcovers.com
The Book Cover Archive - bookcoverarchive.com

Bespoke Book Covers - bespokebookcovers.com

Design Your Own Cover

Of course, you don't have to go elsewhere to get a kickass cover (although it helps). If you're in any way creative when it comes to visuals, and you have a program like Photoshop (and, more importantly, know how to use it), why not try making some of your own covers? Even if you don't end up using any of your designs for your finished book, just the act of creatively putting together images and seeing at least a semi-finished book cover can give you the motivation you need to get writing. Plus, it can be fun!

Play around with different images, colours and themes, and scour the Internet for the perfect font for your book. As I've mentioned with stock photos, fonts come with different licenses, and if you do plan on using it on your actual cover (or website, or any printed material), you will have to purchase the commercial font. Don't worry, though, this doesn't have to break the bank; the most recent font I purchased for commercial use was about £25.

Here are just a few font websites I've used, all of which are listed in the Resources section at the end of the book.

Font Squirrel - www.fontsquirrel.com
DaFont - www.dafont.com
Lost Type - www.losttype.com
The League of Moveable Type -
www.theleagueofmoveabletype.com
Font Monger - www.fontmonger.com

Fonts can make or break a cover, so it's worth spending some time on finding the perfect one for you. Check out some of your favourite authors' book covers first and see what they use (both in terms of fonts, images and colour schemes), and then have a think about what you're trying to convey with your own cover. What genre is this book? Who is it aimed at? What do you want your cover to say to any potential readers? E.g. do you want it to shout out: thriller! Whodunit! Crime! Mystery!? Or do you want it to shout out: comedy! Romance! Holiday read!? You don't have to stick to obvious genre cover stereotypes, of course, but readers like to know what they're getting for their money, and they won't be happy buying a book with a smiling female on the cover, lounging on a beach, if it's about a grisly murder in the heart of London.

It's obvious to stick to genre stereotypes and you may think it's a bit cliché, but sometimes you have to be a bit cliché when it comes to covers just to reel the reader in. We all know the phrase, 'Don't judge a book by its cover', but we also know that when it comes to books, this is exactly what people do, and even more so when buying online; if they're scrolling through several tiny thumbnails on a page listing hundreds of books, they're going to go for the one whose cover pops out at them, and the one that tells them what kind of book they're going to be getting. If you're still not sure, spend some time browsing the Internet for blog posts on covers, or just have a poke around as many categories of books as you can. Of course, for non-fiction, it's a whole different kettle of fish, but the basics are the same: your cover needs to tell the reader what the book's about, and it needs to be eye-catching, with a readable, appropriate font.

If you have fun putting together a 'motivational' cover but don't think it's good enough to use, don't delete it in a hasty moment of self-doubt. Why not use it for something good, and email it to a book designer to show them what you want? Hopefully they'll get the gist of it, and if you already know what images and fonts you want to use, this will make the whole process go a lot quicker and smoother.

Get Inspired By Quotes

If you have a browse on the Internet, there are a million and one inspirational writing quotes that can really help to get you focused and in the mood to write that bestseller. But looking at them once, going, 'ahh yes!' and then immediately forgetting about them doesn't really do you much good. If you find a quote that really strikes a chord with you, copy it into a word document, choose a nice, legible font, and print it out in huge letters. You can then stick this up on the wall where you write (next to your premade book cover, if you decided to do that), so you can stare at it whenever you're feeling those familiar fears and doubts. Some of these quotes will make you think about your own writing, while others will serve to give you a good kick up the arse.

Writing Quotes

After scouring the World Wide Web, here are some of my favourites. Maybe you'll find one of your own favourites too:

"There is nothing to writing. All you do is sit down at a

typewriter and bleed." (Ernest Hemingway)

"If there's a book that you want to read, but it hasn't been written yet, then you must write it." (Toni Morrison)

"If you don't have time to read, you don't have the time (or the tools) to write. Simple as that." (Stephen King)

"We write to taste life twice, in the moment and in retrospect." (Anaïs Nin)

"Fantasy is hardly an escape from reality. It's a way of understanding it." (Lloyd Alexander)

"And by the way, everything in life is writable about if you have the outgoing guts to do it, and the imagination to improvise. The worst enemy to creativity is self-doubt." (Sylvia Plath, *The Unabridged Journals of Sylvia Plath*)

"No tears in the writer, no tears in the reader. No surprise in the writer, no surprise in the reader." (Robert Frost)

"You must stay drunk on writing so reality cannot destroy you." (Ray Bradbury, *Zen in the Art of Writing*)

"Fiction is the truth inside the lie." (Stephen King)

"Don't tell me the moon is shining; show me the glint of light on broken glass." (Anton Chekhov)

"After nourishment, shelter and companionship, stories are the thing we need most in the world." (Philip

Pullman)

"How vain it is to sit down to write when you have not stood up to live." (Henry David Thoreau)

"The scariest moment is always just before you start." (Stephen King, *On Writing: A Memoir of the Craft*)

"Either write something worth reading or do something worth writing." (Benjamin Franklin)

"Writing means sharing. It's part of the human condition to want to share things – thoughts, ideas, opinions." (Paulo Coelho)

"Writing is an exploration. You start from nothing and learn as you go." (E.L. Doctorow)

"Good writing is supposed to evoke sensation in the reader – not the fact that it is raining, but the feeling of being rained upon." (E.L. Doctorow)

"Writing a book of poetry is like dropping a rose petal down the Grand Canyon and waiting for the echo." (Don Marquis)

"While writing, I tend to repeat the same song, endlessly, for thousands of times. This helps me ignore any lyrics, and helps create a consistent mood for each book." (Chuck Palahniuk)

"Prose is architecture, not interior decoration." (Ernest Hemingway)

"To produce a mighty book, you must choose a mighty

theme." (Herman Melville)

"It is perfectly okay to write garbage – as long as you edit brilliantly." (C.J. Cherryh)

"First, find out what your hero wants, then just follow him!" (Ray Bradbury)

"I love deadlines. I like the whooshing sound they make as they fly by." (Douglas Adams)

Thanks to the following websites for these quotes: www.goodreads.com, Brainyquote.com and www.writersdigest.com. These quotes are also listed in the appendix for easy access, if you'd like to print them out and stick them on your wall.

Other Inspirational Quotes

Of course, this doesn't just work with quotes about writing; any inspirational quote can have a motivating effect on you and your work. Here are some of my other favourite quotes that could help you too:

"Put your heart, mind, and soul into even your smallest acts. This is the secret of success." (Swami Sivananda)

"Nothing is impossible, the word itself says 'I'm possible'!" (Audrey Hepburn)

"If opportunity doesn't knock, build a door." (Milton Berle)

"Change your thoughts and you can change your world." (Norman Vincent Peale).

"Believe you can and you're halfway there." (Theodore Roosevelt)

"Follow your bliss and the universe will open doors where there were only walls." (Joseph Campbell)

"Nurture your mind with great thoughts. To believe in the heroic makes heroes." (Benjamin Disraeli)

"Luck is a dividend of sweat. The more you sweat, the luckier you get." (Ray Kroc)

"Either you run the day, or the day runs you." (Jim Rohn)

"Do not go where the path may lead, go instead where there is no path and leave a trail." (Ralph Waldo Emerson)

"The journey of a thousand miles begins with one step." (Lao Tzu)

"We are what we repeatedly do. Excellence, therefore, is not an act but a habit." (Aristotle)

"Dream big and dare to fail." (Norman Vaughan)

"With will one can do anything." (Samuel Smiles)

"Do not wait to strike till the iron is hot; but make it hot by striking." (William B. Sprague)

"Nothing will ever be attempted if all possible objections must first be overcome." (Samuel Johnson)

"Believe with all of your heart that you will do what you were made to do." (Orison Swett Marden)

Thanks to the following websites for these quotes: Brainyquote.com, www.keepinspiring.me and www.inspirational-quotes.info. You can also find these quotes in the appendix.

Creative Ways To Start Creative Writing

Volume Two

by

Jessica Grace Coleman

Get Reading (And Get Involved With) Writer Resources

If you're serious about writing, you've probably already spent hours doing this, but if not, reading writer resources and interviews (both online and in books) can really get you inspired. It's a great way to 'procrastiwork', and by filling your head with information about writing and how others are doing it, you'll be more likely to sit down and get on with your own book.

Online Websites, Forums And Podcasts

First of all, let's take a look at all of the writing resources online – of which there are a lot. This is great as it means we can read about other people's successes and failures and learn from them before we attempt anything ourselves. It's also good for building up our confidence as we learn more about both the craft of writing and the business of selling books.

For example, I initially treated my writing and my books as a hobby – something to do when I had a few spare hours in the evenings or at the weekend, and not as anything that could really make me that much money. I didn't put the time, the effort, or the cash into advertising my books, and as I wasn't serious about it, nothing much happened with them. That was, until I started reading marketing books and started browsing websites for writers – writers who actually made money from their writing!

Soaking up as much knowledge as you can from these kinds of websites (and joining forums and interacting with other members) can not only put you in the writing mood, but can really inspire you to get going after that dream. You're not the only one doing it, and while some will be put off by the idea of all the 'competition', others will utilise these sites, make connections, network, and learn from each other. Here's just a quick list of writing websites, podcasts and forums that can help budding indie writers (all of these will be listed in the Resources section at the end of the book as well for ease):

Kboards - www.kboards.com
The Creative Penn - www.thecreativepenn.com
The Self-Publishing Podcast - selfpublishingpodcast.com
Writer's Beat - www.writersbeat.com
Absolute Write - www.absolutewrite.com
Alliance of Independent Authors - allianceindependentauthors.org
Writing Excuses Podcast - http://www.writingexcuses.com
Grammar Girl - www.quickanddirtytips.com/grammar-girl
Positive Writer - positivewriter.com

This is only a tiny list of thousands of websites, of course, and a quick Google search will get you reading about writing in no time.

Writer Interviews

Another way to spend your time when you're on the web (procrastiworking, not procrastinating, remember – there's a difference) is by reading interviews with your favourite – or new/indie – writers. Not only can these be a wealth of information on the writing process and how to publish, but they can also get you motivated to do your own writing. After all, these people did it, so why can't you?

They can also give you hints and tips on how to do certain writerly things, and you may find some practical help in their wise words. I've probably spent hours and hours of my life reading writer interviews, and every single time, they helped me to get motivated. These authors didn't sit around wallowing in self-doubt and churning out half a novel every six years; they got writing, and they carried on until they were a success. They never gave up, and they always believed in themselves. We can learn a lot from them.

Again, a quick search will throw up thousands of interviews, but here are some ones to start with:

Stephen King Powell's interview - www.powells.com/blog/interviews/the-once-and-future-stephen-king-by-jill/
JK Rowling Amazon interview - www.amazon.com/gp/feature.html?docId=6230
Ian Rankin Writers & Artists interview -

www.writersandartists.co.uk/writers/advice/39/a-writers-toolkit/interviews-with-authors/interview-with-ian-rankin

Terry Pratchett The Telegraph interview - www.telegraph.co.uk/culture/books/authorinterviews/10396286/Terry-Pratchett-interview-a-fantasy-writer-facing-reality.html

Neil Gaiman New Republic interview - www.newrepublic.com/article/115682/neil-gaiman-interview

Toni Morrison Goodreads interview - www.goodreads.com/interviews/show/1029.Toni_Morrison

Dan Brown BookBrowse interview - www.bookbrowse.com/author_interviews/full/index.cfm?author_number=226

Janet Evanovich Internet Writing Journal interview - http://www.writerswrite.com/journal/jan99/a-conversation-with-janet-evanovich-1991

Chuck Palahniuk DVD Talk interview - www.dvdtalk.com/interviews/chuck_palahniuk.html

These interviews are also listed in the Resources section at the end of this book.

Books On Writing

Of course, if you want to have a break and get away from that computer screen (and therefore away from writer resource websites), there are several great books on writing out there that will really inspire you to get going on your own book. These will offer you tips and advice, but generally I find that just by reading them, I'm left with an overwhelming desire to sit down at my computer and let the words flow. The first writing book

I ever read was *On Writing* by Stephen King (I'm a massive King fan), and it's probably one of the best well known, but there are a lot of other great books on the topic too, some of which you may not have heard of.

Here are just a few of the books that could have a positive effect on you, and again they'll be listed in the Resources section in the appendix for ease:

On Writing: A Memoir of the Craft by Stephen King
Zen in the Art of Writing by Ray Bradbury
The War of Art by Steven Pressfield
Writing Down the Bones: Feeling the Writer Within by Natalie Goldberg
The Writing Life by Annie Dillard
How to Write Bestselling Fiction by Dean Koontz
The Elements of Style by William Strunk Jr. and E.B. White

Basically, if you're feeling a bit stuck in the writing stakes but you love (and have the time) to read, reading widely around the subject can be a great motivational tool. This is especially true if you're just starting out and writing seems like something strange and mystical – something unattainable except for a chosen few. Writing is something that anyone (with enough practice) can do – or at least try to do – and reading about how other people do it is a great way of getting into the correct mindset of 'I can do this'. Stop viewing authors as 'the chosen few' and start writing. That's what they did, and look at where they are now! They're writing books about writing! In the future, that could be you – you just have to start.

Get Inspiration From Service Websites

Now, when I say 'service websites', I'm thinking of things like Fiverr, FiverUp, GigBucks, and so on. If you've never used these kinds of sites before, you basically pay an amount (in terms of Fiverr, it's $5, which translates to approximately £3 or just over – bargain!), and someone will provide you with a service, or a 'gig' as they're often called. The amount of stuff on these sites is seemingly endless, but the main areas you'd probably be looking at are listed under things like 'writing & translation', 'graphics & design', 'online marketing', 'advertising' and 'business'. Of course, this is a fun book about fun ways to get creative, so I'll be ignoring the more mundane business-type gigs and focusing on the fun ones.

Cover Promos

The idea of getting book promo graphics made for your novel carries on from the idea of getting your ebook cover designed before you write your book, and I actually did this with the cover for this book. I was about a third of the way through writing the series when I commissioned James at Goonwrite.com to make three covers from a premade one on his site, and as soon as I got it, I headed over to Fiverr and asked one of the graphic designers on there to provide me with a gig that would take that cover and put it into various different set images. I do this for my fiction books as well, and it's quite a rush to see your cover in these images, showing someone reading it on their Kindle in their living room, or looking at it on their iPad while lying on some tropical beach. The 3D book covers are great as well, illustrating how amazing your finished book will look on that shelf or lying on that table in a coffee shop next to a cappuccino. This is brilliant because you don't even need to spend time visualising that finished book – you can see it in the image.

Just as an example, for my £3 something I received five images of my book on various different iPads, and for an extra £3 something I got five more images of my book in 3D book form. The second time I used the service I also got a 'bonus' image, so that's even more bang for your buck. They look great, and you can use these images on your website and social media profiles even before you release your book – get that buzz going. As an aside, one of your images might be put on the seller's gig page, meaning that other prospective buyers of the gig will see it as an example of their work – there's some more free advertising for you. It may not seem like much, but I've actually looked up books and authors from seeing their covers on a Fiverr gig page, so you never know who might see yours.

There are literally hundreds if not thousands of gigs available on these types of sites, so I'll just briefly list some of the other ones here that might come in useful when you're trying to get in that creative writing zone:

Writing & Translation Gigs

This section includes lots of gigs that will help you with your actual writing, if you've got to a bit of a block and are finding it tough to get going again. You can get ghostwriting gigs, proofreading gigs, editing gigs, and copywriting gigs (for example, if you're having trouble writing something for your website). Of course, you won't want your whole book ghostwriting, but you may want a paragraph writing to help you on your way, or you may want a small portion of your writing edited so you can see where you need to improve. After a bit of a look around on Fiverr (again, there are other sites available), some of the more useful gigs include: writing an engaging book blurb (like having a cover, having your blurb ready – even if you don't use those exact words by the time you're finished, can be a great motivational tool), writing a professional biography (again, picturing your author bio on your site and Amazon page can be great inspiration), and writing your book synopsis (if you're not sure where your storyline is going). Yes, some writers may consider this to be 'cheating', but if all of your time is being taken up with writing that masterpiece, you may not have any free time to work on all the extras. You can always rewrite them yourself afterwards, but little bits and pieces like this can help when you're just starting out.

Graphics & Design Gigs

This section offers you a wide variety of lovely designy stuff, whether you need a book cover designing, illustrations drawn for your children's (or other) book, your author website designing, a logo designing for your brand, and so on. There are also fun things like T-shirt design, if you want to start selling merchandise for your book (or if you just want a T-shirt with one of your quotes on, so you can wear it while you're writing and visualise yourself being a success – a success big enough to have your own T-shirt, for example). You can also get flyers and posters designed ready for your book launch, an infographic made to attract people to your blog, and banner ads for your website and social media profiles. You can get business cards and other business stationery designed too, if you want to go down that route. And why not? Getting a brilliantly designed business card with your name and the word 'Author' on it can be a great motivational tool, especially if you hand them out – how embarrassing would it be if you handed out a load of author business cards and then never actually wrote anything? Avoiding embarrassment can be a huge motivator!

Business Gigs

OK, so I said I wouldn't get into all the boring business bits, but there are some fun things in this section too, and some of the fun things include delegating the boring bits to other people – why don't you outsource by getting a virtual assistant, and be done with the jobs you hate? Being a writer is great, but there are always going to be certain tasks that you hate doing, such as updating spreadsheets and doing your books (luckily I love spreadsheets, but doing my taxes is definitely something I pay an accountant for – although not on Fiverr!). Just a quick look at the business section on Fiverr gives me gigs including: doing data entry work, doing Internet research (this could come in handy if you love writing historical novels but hate the time-consuming research part), writing a business plan (useful if you want to actually make money from your writing), and being your virtual assistant (doing all the admin you don't have time to do). It's worth taking a look.

Advertising Gigs

Ah yes, advertising. The part that (most) writers hate, as it often has nothing to do with being creative. Still, if you're serious about making money with your books, you will have to think about this at some point, and knowing that you've got some of it under control (or at least understanding what you need to do) can take the pressure off and allow you to get back to your all-important writing. Looking at websites such as Fiverr can really give you some good ideas, and while some will work better than others, what's £3 to try it? The only thing you're going to lose is £3, which is pretty good when it comes to advertising. This section offers things such as: creating photoshopped images of your book cover/advert on things such as London buses or billboards, using human billboards (yes, you read that right), handing out flyers in towns and cities all over the world (although make sure you ask for photographic evidence if you choose one of these gigs), and creating ads for radio shows and for use on blogs. OK, yes, some of these won't get you very far compared with other advertising campaigns (such as Google Adwords), but it can be fun to get some mocked-up ads, and thinking of your book flyers being given out all over the world can be a bit of a thrill too (of course, you should wait until after you've finished your book to do this).

Other Gigs

The 'Music & Audio' section will let you create adverts and jingles for radio, TV, and the Internet, and in terms of books, things like book trailers can be a good way of motivating yourself to carry on writing. You can pay people to do voiceovers and sound effects, as well as doing singing for you if you want to create something original for your book trailer or promotional YouTube video. Similarly, 'Video & Animation' can help you create mini adverts for your books, whether you want to use animation, actors, or puppets (yes, puppets – both Sesame Street type puppets and creepy ventriloquist dummies). 'Programming & Tech' can help you with websites such as WordPress sites, mobile apps, and any other technology-based things you need to do in order to get your name out there. Again, having an author website (even before you release your book) can be a great motivator.

There are also the more random sections on sites like Fiverr, such as 'gifts', 'lifestyle', 'fun & bizarre' and 'other'. I'm not saying any of these will help you with your quest to be an author, but there are some pretty fun things you could do to help you get in the zone. For example, one gig offers to 'answer a psychic question by tea leaf reading'. Stuck on a plot point? Not sure whether to make your main character do something or not? Ask the tea leaves! I'm not even joking – sometimes, when you've got a writing brain block, you'll try anything to get your answer, so you may as well leave it up to the tea gods over anything else. You can also get weight loss programmes and diet and nutrition advice (always useful, as you need a healthy mind to concentrate on writing, and exercise can give you those all-important endorphins that will leave you feeling positive about your future writing career, instead of stressing over whether you should be a writer at all). There are subject matter experts on there who can answer your questions on police procedure and medical conditions – or whatever else you're writing about – and you can even pay someone to 'be a good friend' if you have any issues you'd like to talk through (yes, this is really a thing, and who knows? It could come in useful. After all, being an author is a lonely career sometimes). The gifts section can also be pretty fun, as there are a lot of people offering personalised objects, things you could use as promotional items or prizes for competitions involving your writing. You just need to think outside the box, but don't go too crazy on these sites – before you know it, you'll have spend hundreds of pounds just on the 'fun & bizarre' section.

It's worth noting here that although it sounds amazing that you can get all these services for $5/£3 each, there are some catches. A lot of gigs will have this set fee, but sometimes you will only get a basic service for this amount, and will have to pay more money for 'gig extras' to get what you need. These extras can include the same service but with a much faster turnaround, extra versions of the gig so you can choose between them, and so on. Spend some time browsing the site, though, and you're bound to find a gig that suits you. And for £3, it's hardly going to break the bank if you pay for something and end up not liking it. Experiment, buy a few gigs, and see what you get. You can use the rating system to see how many other people recommend a particular gig, and look at the examples on their page to see work they've done before for an idea of what you'll be getting.

I've used Fiverr for several things over the years – most

recently, some 3D promo pictures of my books on iPads and paperbacks – and it's always quite exciting to see an email in your inbox telling you that your 'gig' is ready (yes, I'm that sad). Just looking around sites like these and seeing what's available in terms of helping you write, helping you design books, and helping you market those books can give you some great inspiration and motivation to sit down and write.

Ways To Write

I'm sure you're aware that these days, there are literally hundreds of different ways you can actually start writing, whether you rely on technology or want to start out old skool, with a trusty notebook and pen. I'm going to go through these briefly, as this book is really about how to get in the creative mindset than how to actually write your masterpiece, but I think it's worth running through them if you're a first time writer. After all, if you're spending all your time researching what programs to use, you're leaving yourself very little time to actually get creative, so hopefully this will help.

Technology

Now, I know that when you're trying to get into the creative zone, it can be best to ditch the technology and look at other ways of finding your mojo, but the truth is, there are so many helpful apps, programs and websites that it may be worth your while to stay on that computer – or that tablet or phone – a while longer. The main thing is that you get away from that blank document, away from the word processor, and into things that will get you thinking differently about your project.

The following apps and sites have been made with the intention of helping writers get on with their craft. Some I have tried, some I have used (and use regularly), and some I've simply seen recommended. You need to find the right piece of technology for you, and of course, you can play around with some of these (particularly the ones that are free or cheap) to see if they do help you with your writing. Some are little fun things that don't take a lot of brain power to use (which is good if you're currently suffering from 'fried brain syndrome' after staring at your document for so long), whereas others require a little more getting used to before you can get the best use out of them.

It is worth noting here again that I am not being paid to recommend any products over others, these are simply the ones I'm aware of and that I think have some value when getting into the creative mindset. There are hundreds if not thousands of alternatives – just search for things like 'creative writing' and 'novel help' in your app store of choice to see more.

Word Processor

Ah, the trusty word processor. The most common one is Word, of course, and this is how I wrote my first five novels and my first short story collection. I'd used Word for years, through high school and then university, and I felt comfortable with it – it was familiar and it was easy; you just sat down and typed. It was only after I'd written most of those books that I started to realise it wasn't, in fact, the only way you could write a book, and after several different recommendations from various author friends, I decided to check them out. Of course, one main advantage of Word is that if you've already got Microsoft Office, you don't need to shell out for another program or subscription. It is possible to create good ebook templates and paperback layouts in Word, although it can be a little tricky and annoying to do some things in it. If you have no other options, Word is more than fine, and for some people, it's a case of the simpler, the better. You won't need to learn any new skills (or not many, anyway), and you won't have to read instruction books just to know how to work it.

Scrivener

Developed by Literature and Latte, this little program is really nifty. You can download a free trial so you can see if you like it before you buy, and then it's around £35 if you decide you do like it – and you probably will. There's just so much you can do with it, from planning your novel, keeping track of scenes, locations and characters, writing your book, and then compiling it into ebooks of many different types, as well as typesetting it for paperback formatting. A lot of writers love the corkboard in Scrivener – using little virtual post-its to set out their scenes, keeping track of their characters, and generally organising their novel in a fun and visual way. Everything's linked, so you can set up your little notes on the corkboard for your storyline, then if you move the notes around, the scenes will move around in your draft.

There's also the 'Outliner', which allows you to plan in a different way, and you can set yourself targets so you can keep on track with your writing schedule – for example, set a word count of 5,000 per chapter, or so many characters per scene. This will make you more aware of the amount of words you're writing, which could be a good thing, but could also be pretty bad if you're not very prolific. Still, that doesn't matter – just do a few of the exercises in this book and then go back to it. By this point, hopefully you'll be in the zone and can blast that word count target out of the water!

Compiling manuscripts into different formats is incredibly easy on Scrivener. I use it to create mobi files for the Kindle, something that saves a lot of time and swearing at the computer compared to when I used to try and do it on my own using a word processor. I also use it to create pdf files and epub files, for when I'm giving away a free book and have to give readers different options depending on how they want to read it (on the computer, on their Kindle, on another e-reader device or app, and so on). You can play around with the different settings to get your ebook exactly how you want it to look, and if you're creating mobi files for the Kindle on the Amazon store, it will generate your table of contents for you. Copying elements from one Scrivener file to another is really easy too – just have both projects open and drag things across. I do this for my front and end matter of a book, where I have my copyright page and 'Also By Jessica Grace Coleman' pages.

Scrivener basically just makes everything much, much easier, and spending a few hours getting to grips with it (and reading about it) will be a brilliant investment of your time. It has completely changed the way I write books, and it definitely saves me a lot of time when it comes to putting my manuscript into different formats. The more you play around with it, the more cool features you'll find, so it's definitely worth at least the free trial to see how it can revolutionise your own writing.

You can also use Scrivener for writing non-fiction and doing scriptwriting, and there are hundreds of tutorial videos and websites out on the World Wide Web to help you when you're getting to grips with the software. I also recommend *Scrivener For Dummies* if you want to spend some time away from the computer and wish to learn more about the program. You can get Scrivener from literatureandlatte.com.

Final Draft

A lot of people think that Final Draft is only for screenwriters, and while it is brilliant for this, you can also use it for several other types of work, from regular text documents to graphic novels and more. If you are thinking of screenwriting, Final Draft is the program to use – seemingly everyone in the industry uses it (including all the top Hollywood directors and producers), so in that way it is 'industry standard', and just by using it, you're putting yourself in the same league as all those guys (well, we've all got to start somewhere).

While we're talking about Final Draft, if you're finding a novel hard to start, why not begin writing your book as a screenplay? You don't have to actually write a screenplay, or do many scenes, but thinking about how your characters would act and move around can really help you get into their mindset, which in turn can help you with your novel. Also, if you've already written a novel, you can try turning it into a screenplay as a writing exercise, even if you don't plan on ever doing anything with it. Who knows? You might find a passion for screenwriting that you didn't know you had, and even if you don't, it can be a great way of learning more about the art of writing.

Write Or Die

Write Or Die is a fun little program – putting the 'Prod' in productivity, as they say. It basically allows you to set a time limit for yourself, and then the idea is you sit down and write, and if you stop writing before you reach your time limit… you die. OK, so that doesn't actually happen – what does happen is you get 'punished' for not writing – but it really is a great tool for getting into the writing mindset. There are several settings you can have it on, from gentle (you'll just get a reminder to keep writing), to normal (you'll hear a rather unpleasant sound – as long as you've got your speakers turned up) and Kamikaze, which I think is a bit of evil genius. In this mode, if you don't keep consistently writing, your work will start to unwrite itself in front of your very eyes – a writer's worst nightmare. The idea, apparently, is to give the writer a fear: a fear of *not* writing. This won't work for everyone, and some people will get so stressed out they might want to start attacking their computer, but it's a fun little exercise to try out. Write or Die is available as an app, and there's also a desktop edition for you to use on your computer. Give it a go and see how you react in Kamikaze mode!

Tablet Apps

Of course, sometimes you don't have easy access to laptops and computers, or you might want to carry on with your writing while you're away and don't want to lug your laptop around with you. I'm a bit of an Apple addict, so as well as my Macbook and my iPhone, I also have an iPad, which comes in very handy when I'm away from my computer. If I need to type something, I'll use Pages on my iPad, which is easier to use if you have an attached keyboard, but not impossible without one, and you can even use the dictation option if you don't want to fiddle about with the keys. I actually started writing this book using Pages on my iPad (after I'd accidentally thrown a smoothie on my old laptop and was waiting for my shiny new one to arrive), using a mix of the onscreen keyboard and the dictation facility.

You can also get other word processing programs for your iPad, and HanxWriter (a virtual typewriter) is pretty fun to use as well (it comes with the very satisfying old typewriter noises, including the carriage return – yes, I know I'm a geek). They keys on HanxWriter are actually pretty big too, so it's not as fiddly as you might think. Werdsmith is another writing app, where you can list your projects and ideas, and IndexCard emulates the corkboard on Scrivener. There are numerous other apps, from StorySkeleton to Playwriter, and Story Planner for Writers to Word Keeper. You can get most of these on your phone too (although that will be majorly fiddly), but remember to check the reviews before you commit to buying anything.

Notebook And Pen

Of course, some people are happiest when all they have to work with is a notebook and pen. Take away all of the fancy computer programs and devices, and all you're left with is a blank page, waiting to be filled with your scribbles. If you've never tried to write a big project using just a notebook and pen, it can be worth giving it a go. Even if you just write a few pages and then type them up straight away, sometimes the act of stepping away from the glowing computer screen and going old skool can be all you need to reset your brain.

There are other advantages to the ole' pen and paper method too – it doesn't matter if your laptop throws a hissy fit and shuts down, and you can write anywhere: in the garden, in a café (I don't know about you, but the thought of taking my nice shiny laptop into a place filled with hot drinks just waiting to be dropped all over the keys and the screen makes me go cold inside), and when commuting on trains or other public transport. It can often be easier to pull out a notepad and pen than it is to set up a computer, and again, the 'freedom' of writing by hand can really help if you're used to sitting and hitting keys. Just make sure you don't leave your notepad on the bus or in a café, or you might soon be reading a bestseller by someone whose words closely resemble your own..!

Typewriter

If you're feeling particularly retro, there's always the trusty old typewriter – if you can find one that still works. Of course, this probably isn't a way to write your entire novel (unless you really don't have any other way of doing it), but it can be a fun way to start. And like I said, if you don't have one, just get the HanxWriter app to pretend you do have one!

Dictation

I can't help but feel this particular idea might be a better recommendation a few years into the future, but right now, you can still get some decent dictation programs that can help you with getting words onto the page – if you can't face typing. For some people, I think the creative mental block has to do with the actual act of putting your fingers on the keys and creating sentences with your words, something which dictation eliminates in the first instance.

Now, we all know that the first draft is meant for you to simply write – without worrying about editing – but that's easier said than done. Most of us have an innate desire and urge to edit as we type, to finish sentences properly and not to trail off mid-sentence or use incorrect grammar. Over the years I've got used to pretty much just 'vomit typing' onto the page, not caring for misspelled words or dodgy punctuation, but to start with it took me ages to complete my first draft because I wanted it to be perfect. The sooner you get out of that mindset the better, as you'll speed up a lot when you realise you can just spew words forth onto your document and deal with cleaning it all up, nice and neatly, later on.

Even with treating the first draft like this, however, some writers still find it difficult to start getting those words – even if they're bad words – onto the page. So, one way of combating this is by using dictation software, as while we may find typing a story hard, most of us can waffle on to ourselves about potential story ideas with no problem. This might be best tried for the first time when you're on your own in the house (or wherever you write) as it can feel a little silly while you try and get the right pace and volume of your voice, but talking at your computer (or phone, or tablet) can be quite fun. It can also be quite funny when the software gets your words wrong – 'she entered the room, her heart pounding in her chest and her forehead sweating in the cool air' can inexplicably change to 'she evil room founding her pressed four head swearing elephant tobacco palm tree', but like I said, it will probably improve in the future and it will also depend on what program you're using. Plus, you still have words on the page that you can edit later, they'll just be slightly more random words than you were hoping for – maybe there'd even be a story in there somewhere, if you look very, very closely!

You can spend hundreds of pounds on dictation software, and as I haven't tried any of the more expensive options, I can't review them one way or the other, but you can get cheaper options if you just want to use it as a way of getting some – any! – words down on the page. I have Dragon Dictation on my phone, which is a bit hit and miss, and I've also started using the dictation option on Pages (Apple products) and also Word (Office for the Mac, in my case). These can be pretty good, and if you're going to go through and edit it afterwards anyway, it doesn't really matter if there are a few wrong words here and there. Sometimes (especially if you're tired and trying to get some novel work in at the end of a long day at work), it's easier just to collapse on the sofa and talk at your computer instead of trying to form your fingers into useful typing digits. It's at least quite fun to experiment with, anyway, even if you don't end up using it that much.

I wrote some of the first draft of this book using Pages then Word dictation, and it helped to have a mix of writing and typing. Needless to say, we're strictly talking first drafts here – don't try and publish anything straight away after using dictation software, unless you want people to think you spout off gibberish in the middle of sentences. Some lines will even make it sound like you were a bit – or a lot – tipsy when writing. I suppose you could say it was a stylistic quirk, but other than that, stick to dictation for the first draft only.

Here are some links to the apps and software mentioned in this section, and these are also listed in the Resources page in the appendix:

Microsoft Word - www.microsoftstore.com
Scrivener - www.literatureandlatte.com
Final Draft - www.finaldraft.com
Write Or Die - writeordie.com
Apple Pages - www.apple.com/uk/mac/pages/
HanxWriter - www.hitcents.com/b2b/work/hanx
Werdsmith - werdsmith.com
IndexCard - www.denvog.com/app/index-card/
StorySkeleton - www.storyskeleton.com
Story Planner for Writers - www.literautas.com/en/apps/story-planner-for-writers-app-outline-your-novel/
Word Keeper - www.preapps.com/new-iphone-ipad-apps/word-keeper-track-writing-progress-with-timer-charts-and-stats-for-author-writer-and-student/3034
Microsoft Excel - www.microsoftstore.com

Tools To Help You Concentrate

Even if you're deep in the creative zone and you've done everything you can to get to the point where you're ready to start writing, there's still the little tiny thing called concentration – how do you get it? And once you've got it, how do you keep it for the whole writing session? Here are some tools, and yes, some are a little silly, but why not give them a shot?

Earplugs

I have weird ears, I admit it. I can never wear in-ear headphones, as they just slip right out, and because of this I never thought I'd be able to wear earplugs (just bear with me, I do have a point here). When I first started writing properly, I lived with my parents out in the country, and the most noise you'd ever hear would be sheep bleating in the field or birds cheeping outside your window. They were nice country noises, noises that actually helped inspire me to write (as at that point I was writing about a group of people who lived in the country). There weren't many other houses in the direct area, and there weren't any kids or arguing couples. When I moved, however, the sounds changed. I didn't move to an inner city flat or anything – I moved to a townhouse in a nice estate near the town centre – but it was enough. The house is close to a lot of other houses where there are a lot of kids, and it's pretty close to a retail park where lorries and all sorts come and go all the time. Not to mention all the roadworks that took place on the estate, with the sound of drills drilling into your brain, and on occasion, the house shaking as a digger did its thing or as a train went by in the distance.

It suddenly became quite a lot harder to concentrate on my writing, and while sometimes I could listen to soothing music (as long as it had no lyrics that would sneakily make their way into my manuscript without me realising), at other times I needed absolute silence. Now, for normal people with normal ears, this would be quite easy – just pop some cheapo foam earplugs in and you're grand. For me, I had to do a little more research, and I found a magical website where all your earplug needs could be met, even if you have strange shaped ears. The site is www.snorestore.co.uk and it's helped me a lot. You can buy a taster pack for about £14 that includes a set of each of the earplugs they do, and you can try them out until you find some that work.

I found some silicon ones that mould to your ear shape, and I was amazed when I tried them to find that a) they didn't fall out and b) they actually worked. It was like being in a soundless vacuum, not something everyone will like but something that definitely works for me. I began using these when I was writing, and then I began using them when I was sleeping. The first night I used them I think I had the best night's sleep I've ever had, which of course is something else you need to consider when trying to be creative: if you're constantly knackered, you're not going to be producing your best work. So, get some earplugs, get some sleep, and get some work done. Strange earplug bit over.

Tea

Like many British people, I am an avid believer in the power of tea, and no I'm not even joking. Not a single day goes by (even in the summer – which, let's face it, doesn't mean much in England) where I don't have at least a couple of cups of tea, and I'm very much of the opinion that a cup of tea will help in almost any situation. I'll have tea to wake me up, tea to get into the work zone, tea to relax, tea to make me feel better when I'm ill, and tea to commiserate with when I've had a bad day. I drink good old builder's tea and strange-sounding herbal teas, and my favourite one to relax with (in case you were wondering) is Celestial Seasonings' Sleepytime tea with vanilla.

But what about writing? I almost always have a nice cup of tea before I sit down to write – possibly with a tiny bit of sugar in if I'm not very awake – and I've done it so many times now that the very act of putting on the kettle and sitting down at my desk with a brew helps me get in the right headspace. Of course, it doesn't have to be tea – choose your own favourite drink. A lot of writers swear by coffee for obvious reasons, and some even do their first draft writing with a nice glass of wine on standby (if you're thinking the same thing, just make sure you don't do your editing while drinking a glass of wine or two – it probably won't end well). I find tea soothing, and therefore I find that it helps me concentrate. This may be more of a psychosomatic thing than a physical response, but either way, it works, so that's good enough for me. In fact, I think it might be time for another cup of tea...

Music

Music is mentioned elsewhere in this book, but if you're the kind of person who can write while listening to music, it's a good idea to listen to the same thing (or the same artist if one song gets boring) before you sit down and write. Do it every time and don't skip it. Once your mind associates that song with sitting down and getting words on the page, it'll help you to get into the right headspace, and hopefully, it should get to the point where even just hearing the start of that song will focus your mind and make you want to write. Of course, some people will be more susceptible to this than others, but why not give it a try? If you don't have much 'relaxing' music, take a look at the playlists/categories on Spotify. I talk about some of these in the 'Creative Playlists' section in the appendix.

Finding A Good Writing Space

In today's fast-paced world, when there's always something going on no matter where you are, it can be seemingly impossible to find a space where you can sit quietly and work. It is, however, essential. If you can claim somewhere (whether it's an office, a spare room, the garage, or a cupboard under the stairs) to sit and write, and where you can keep going back to sit and write, your brain will start associating that place with – you got it – writing, and with being productive. If you use your living room to relax with the family and watch TV and films in, you might not find it the best place to get into the writing headspace.

Of course, people are all different, and whereas one writer might need absolute silence in order to work, another might actually like the hustle and bustle of their favourite coffee shop, or the constant streaming traffic of family members coming in and out of the kitchen while you write at the kitchen table. Find what works for you, and stick to it. Many people find that leaving the house before they get to work puts them in the right frame of mind, so if you can work from a café, a friend's house, or a hired desk in a shared office, this might help you separate your writing from your free time. Perhaps you have a summer house, shed or garage you can sit in and work – sometimes leaving the house by just a few steps is enough to reset your brain and tell it you're going to get in the writing zone. Other options include a caravan (if you have one – it's probably not a good idea to start using other people's caravans), the loft (unless it's full of rubbish and spiders, in which case it's not going to be a good writing environment for anyone), or maybe even random spaces in your house like a utility room. Just find a space and stick to it, and your writing will thank you.

Starting Off Small (Or Just Differently)

If launching yourself into a long, complicated novel fills you with an insane fear, why not stop, take a step back, and try something else first? Taking baby steps could be your way 'in' to the creative writing zone, and here are a few ideas of how to take them.

Poetry And Haikus

One way of getting into writing without starting with a lengthy novel is by writing poetry (or haikus, if a poem seems like too much). This, of course, is a completely different discipline to writing prose, but I find it can really help with getting in the creative mindset.

Poems come in all shapes and sizes, and you can write either a completely random one just to get you into the creative zone, or one that incorporates ideas and characters from the book you want to write. You could even do one per scene or per chapter of your novel to get you going, and it doesn't have to be poetically brilliant either – if you're the only one who's going to be reading it, what does it matter?

Why not write a poem about one of your main characters? Or a poem describing the main location for the book? Perhaps you could put one of your main scenes into poetry form? Now, I'm awful at poetry, and the most I ever write are really simple rhyming couplets, but I find it fun, and it does start to loosen up your brain ready for your big writing project.

And who knows? You might find a passion for poetry and start writing a poetry collection instead of (or as well as) your novel. In the same vein, reading poetry can be soothing and can help get you in the creative mindset to start writing.

Short Stories

If you're trying to write your first novel but are finding it hard to get into (after all, a 70,000+ word full-length novel is daunting to anyone), short stories can be the way to go. Why not try writing a short story about elements of your novel? Or perhaps turn an upcoming scene into a story of its own – by looking at it as a short story rather than a small piece of a much bigger novel, you might be able to trick your brain into not freaking out quite as much. Even better, try some flash fiction. These can be really, really short, but they still have the same purpose – it will get you writing, and that's the main thing, especially if you've been suffering from a creative blockage. More on this in the next section.

Short stories can help get you into the writing zone, and you can use them to explore themes, settings and characters that you'll be writing about in your novel. For example, write the opening of the book as a short story, or one or two of the scenes from later on in the novel. While there's some debate about this, short stories are usually around the 1,000 to 10,000 word mark, although there are also novelettes and novellas as well at higher word counts. If you're not writing short stories to publish (or may eventually end up self-publishing them in a collection), then it doesn't matter too much about the word count; just try and write one short story and take it from there. If you can write a short story, you can write a novella, and if you can write a novella, you can write a novel. If you can write a novel, you can write a series… you get the idea. We all have to start somewhere.

Flash Fiction

If you're in the frame of mind when even short stories seem like too much effort, perhaps aim a little lower to begin with and write a piece of flash fiction. These are generally under 1,000 words, and can be as few as 50 words or less. (Think of Hemingway's six word story – 'For sale: baby shoes, never worn.') Writing flash fiction can be hard, and it is definitely at the opposite end of the scale to writing a full-blown novel, but both will give you more writing skills than you had before, and it can be fun trying to fit a story into so few words. Try it now, and if you're not sure what you're meant to be doing, check out some of the flash fiction collections available as ebooks. Because of their lengths, they're usually pretty cheap.

Whatever you do, think small, get it written, and then move on to something a bit bigger. Eventually, you'll be able to tackle that novel with no problems whatsoever (well, in terms of getting into the creative zone; I can't promise that your plot holes will magically fill themselves in or that your characters won't go and get themselves into trouble!). Sometimes, we all just need to start off a little slowly.

Reading

This can be a bit of a controversial method to starting your own writing – as you don't want to subconsciously start stealing other writers' styles or ideas – but generally, reading books on a similar subject or of the same genre as your own can help. It can have the opposite effect as well, of course – you might end up weeping about how good their books are and how yours will never be that good – but most of the time, I find it useful. Obviously, you need to know your genre anyway, so you should have read as many of the similar books out there as you can, but actually reading them while writing your own can result in the transferral (whether you know it or not) of at least some aspects of their work. If you're simply using it as inspiration, great, but if your writing starts to sound the same and your dialogue seems remarkably similar, it may be time to stop reading that book – at least until you're finished.

When I was starting my YA sci-fi novel, I read as much as I could of popular books in that genre. It got me in the right mood, and I knew the kind of thing I was aiming for, but as I want to put my own twist on the genre, I'm not reading those kinds of books as I'm actually writing it – I don't want to risk subconsciously using anyone else's ideas, but I also want to make sure that my voice is my own, and that I put my own spin on the genre and the story.

In general, I read as many different genres and types of

books as I can, in order to expand my knowledge and improve my own writing by seeing how others write. For instance, I read autobiographies as I write/edit a lot of life stories in my day job, but I also read crime novels and westerns, ghost stories and marketing books. I read Stephen King and Charles Dickens and Charlaine Harris – all kinds of different writers and all kinds of different genres. I really think this helps your writing, and once I start a book, I always, always finish it, even if I'm not that into it – I do this because I think there's always something you can learn from books (no matter what that lesson is), and because as a writer myself, I know how much hard work will have gone into each and every book. Someone has poured their heart and soul into that book, spent endless hours typing away, and not even sleeping some nights while they stay up and edit their work before going back to their 'real' job in the morning. Just because it's not my cup of tea, doesn't mean I don't appreciate the effort that's gone into it. So I read widely, and I always finish what I start. Reading – no matter what it is – can be a good break from your computer screen, a way of learning about the craft, and a way of getting some (but not too much) inspiration for your own work.

If reading about different things gets in the way of you writing your own story, you can always read about reading for some quick inspiration. Goodreads is a great place for this: you can mix with like-minded literary enthusiasts, and you can discuss the kinds of books that are out there right now. Reading about people enthusing about reading always gets me motivated – just think: you could be the next person they enthuse about. There's nothing quite like word of mouth praise, and thinking of yourself and your own books being listed on those kinds of websites is a good motivational tool as well.

Finding Motivation Online

I've mentioned this briefly under other topics, but you really can't underestimate the Internet as a source of writing inspiration, especially when it comes to other writers. Knowing that there are other people out there going through exactly the same thing you are (especially if you're having trouble getting into that pesky creative zone) can be a big help, and there are tons of places online where you can find writers who you can strike up a conversation with. Start with Twitter and Facebook and other social media sites, then progress onto online writing groups, writing forums, and writing blogs that have a big following. Glean as much information as you can, because knowledge is power, and you'll probably get inspired by all the writers you start reading about and interacting with. Plus, it's nice to be a part of a community, isn't it?

Writing Groups (Online And In Real Life)

As you probably already know, writing can be a lonely profession, especially if it's your only profession. You usually work from home, seeing hardly anyone but your family and maybe the postman for days at a time. You might go an entire workweek without leaving the house (this is scarily easy to do when you're focused on a project), and you might feel like you're starting to wither away with no proper exposure to daylight and no interaction with actual people (this is especially true if you live alone, of course). Days blur into each other, then the weeks blur into each other, and before you know it, you're getting to the end of yet another year. Scary stuff, but it happens.

One way of getting through this is by acquainting yourself with other people who are doing the same thing as you, and by that I mean: writers. If you don't have any friends in the 'real world' who are writers, then make some – either online or in person (and sometimes, your online friends can become your friends in real life). There are several different ways of doing this, and you might already have done some of these when setting up your author platform online. For example, if you have a Twitter or Facebook profile for you as an 'author', you've probably liked and followed other authors and people in the publishing industry in order to get likes and follows back, and so you can learn from what they have to say. The same goes for LinkedIn, Google Plus, and tons of other social networking sites.

This networking is great for building up your online presence (something you can do before you even release your first book), but it's also great for 'meeting' people with the same profession (or hobby) as you. Ask them for advice, help them out when they ask you for advice, and generally just strike up a friendship. Having someone to talk to who is facing the same dilemmas as you can be extremely helpful, especially if you're in exactly the same boat (e.g. on track to self-publish your first novel, writing in your spare time but hoping to earn money from it in the future). Suddenly, writing won't feel like such a lonely thing to do, and if you get stuck, you know who you can turn to.

As well as making friends on social networking sites, you can also join online readers' and writers' groups, so you'll have a whole host of people to talk to when you need help, or when you get bored, or when you just need to speak to *someone* other than yourself (or your cat). I'm part of several writing and reading groups on Facebook, which is an easy place to start, or you can do a quick online search to find a group that appeals to you.

If talking online to people (and therefore, spending even more time at your screen) doesn't appeal, and if you just need to get out of that house, then perhaps the real life version of these groups would be better for you. This search may start online, but once you've found a group in your area, you could soon be going to monthly, fortnightly or weekly meetings to discuss things you love. You can also use these groups to get feedback on your novel (which can be a scary thought, but something that will be worth it in the end) and it can also help to see where other writers are with their projects, and the kinds of problems they've come across. Who knows? You might end up actually liking the people in these groups, giving your social life a new angle – people to socialise with who will also help you with your writing/your career. It's the best of both worlds.

Now, some people will understandably be a little apprehensive about joining a new group – especially if it's one you found out about online – but if you don't try it, you won't find out how good or how helpful it could be. The obvious rules about meeting up with someone you don't know apply – go with a friend if you're anxious, meet in a public place, tell someone where you're going and so on – but if it's a group of people who already have a positive presence online, you should be fine.

So, where do you start looking for a local group? A general search will no doubt throw up a few potential answers, but there are several websites that will help you out much quicker – both writing sites and local interest sites. Don't be afraid to send out a message on Facebook or Twitter asking if anyone knows of any local groups, and signing up to community websites such as Streetlife can be a good source of local information as well. Meetup is also a great website for local groups of all kinds. For example, if you work from home and miss the social interaction of an office, you can find a group of people who work from home, and who meet up occasionally to get out of the house – either working together or taking a break to have a coffee and a catch up. Get out the house and make new friends in one fell swoop.

Of course, the main point of this book is getting into the creative zone, and having discussions with like-minded people can help you do that. Just think how good it must feel to talk to someone who's been through exactly what you're going through, and who not only finished their first novel, but also went on to write another and another, self-publish them all, and make money from them. They did it, and so can you. It's great motivation, and it's great for getting you unstuck from your current writing blockage. Plus, if you're meeting people in real life, you can leave the computer at home for a few hours while you go out and reset your brain. A few hours in a café (or better yet, a pub if you have the occasional tipple) can work wonders, and surrounding yourself with positive people who share your interests and dreams can make you want to go after your own.

Here are some websites that could help you in your quest for making writer friends, both online and in person (these are also listed in the Resources section at the end of the book):

Write Words Writers' Groups - www.writewords.org.uk/groups
Great Writing - www.greatwriting.co.uk
UK Writers' College List of Writing Circles in the UK - www.ukwriterscollege.co.uk/Writing+Resources/UK+Writers+College++Writing+Circles.html
Writers Online List of Writing Groups - www.writers-online.co.uk/Writers-Groups/
Scribeophile Writing Group - www.scribophile.com
Facebook - www.facebook.com
Streetlife - www.streetlife.com
Meetup - www.meetup.com

Writing Courses (Online And In Real Life)

Writing courses can be a great way to give yourself that kick up the arse you need. You don't have to get a degree or a diploma (although you can if you want to), and you don't have to physically go to any courses or workshops (although, again, you can if you want to). The easiest and quickest way to do it is to take part in an online course, either by yourself (by downloading the lessons and going through them on your own) or with other people (interacting with other students in your class by using online groups). I've done courses both ways.

They don't just have to be writing courses, either – you can do courses on the subjects you're writing about. For instance, I've done solo courses on creative writing and screenplay writing, but I've also done them on criminology and forensics. You can usually find most of the information used in these courses for free online, but a lot of people find it easier and quicker to just sit down and complete a course that is already written and waiting for them to read. And they don't have to cost the earth, either – you can often find great deals on Groupon for all kinds of courses (including a lot of business ones, which can help with your writing, especially if you're trying to make money from it), often for just £10 - £20. There are also free online course sites (such as ALISON and FutureLearn), though I've never tried any of these myself so I can't tell you if they're any good.

I've also paid a lot more for courses. In fact, the first online course I ever did was an Introduction to Creative Writing distance-learning course with Oxford University. It cost a few hundred pounds, but I actually got some credits from the course (or CATS points as they're called at the Uni), and if you do several courses, you can actually put it towards a university credit. I liked that idea – plus the fact that it was Oxford – and as it was ten weeks long, I felt like I was getting my money's worth. We had our own class, our own forum on the university continuing education website, and our own tutor, whom we could email or chat to online if we had any questions. We had assignments and grades, and

I really felt like I learned a lot.

More importantly than that, however, was the fact that it got me thinking about the writing I actually wanted to do. It was after this course that I started planning my first novel, *The Former World*, and if I hadn't gone on it, I really don't know if I would have started writing properly or not. Before that, although I'd done well at writing at school, and although a couple of teachers had told me I should pursue writing, I didn't feel like I really had any right to just start randomly writing a novel. It may sound stupid, but after doing that course, I got it in my head that actually, maybe I *could* just start randomly writing a novel. Everyone's got to start somewhere, and now I had at least some form of writing education behind me. It gave me the push I needed, and to this day I still think it's probably one of the best few hundred pounds I've ever spent, because it set me on my path to where I am now.

Here are just a few options, also listed in the Resources section in the appendix:

Groupon - www.groupon.co.uk
Oxford University Continuing Education – Online & Distance Learning -
http://www.ox.ac.uk/admissions/continuing-education/online-and-distance-courses
ALISON - alison.com
FutureLearn - www.futurelearn.com
The Writers' Workshop - www.writersworkshop.co.uk
UEA Creative Writing Online Courses -
https://www.uea.ac.uk/literature/creative-writing/creative-writing-online

Games And Socialising Online

Online, social networking games can be a good way of taking your mind off your writing for a few minutes, and they can even – if you're playing a game like Scrabble – help your vocabulary, which is always good for writers. If you're playing these over social network sites like Facebook, there's also the 'social' element – something which is also good for writers as we often live solitary work lives, writing on our own and away from other people. So get playing, and get interacting with people – feeling connected to others is important, even if it's just talking to someone on Facebook or Twitter.

I use Facebook chat quite a lot, especially with my editor friends who help me out with Coleman Editing, and as we're based so far away from each other, we can create a kind of 'virtual office' where we can go and talk to each other, either about work or about other, more random things. If you're serious about writing and have got writer friends (either online or in real life), why not create a group chat on Facebook that you can dip in and out of during the day? You'll feel less isolated and you can ask their opinions on parts of your writing as you go.

Crowdfunding Sites

I think crowdfunding sites (such as Kickstarter) are great, whether you're trying to get a project off the ground or you just want to be involved in someone else's project. I'm signed up to Kickstarter, and I'll occasionally browse through the projects (books and others) to see if I want to put some money into something. I don't usually put a lot, but you don't *have* to put a lot – the minimum is usually £5/$5. It's a great way of showing your support for something, and depending on how much money you donate, you'll get 'rewards', such as a signed copy of the book or your name listed in the acknowledgements.

For example, I put some money into a project, and my name was listed inside the book. I didn't donate enough to receive a copy of the book from the writer, but as I knew my name was in there – and as I knew, in some small way, I'd helped to get that book published – I wanted a copy anyway, so I bought it and read it. It's great to feel a part of something, and you could even try listing your own project on there if you think there'll be enough interest (there can be quite a lot of competition, but as with most things in life, if you don't give it a go, you'll never know). If you do invest in a literary project, you can get a good insight into the process, as the author will email you updates throughout so you can see how long it takes to write, then edit, then sort out all the extra bits at the end in order to get the completed book.

So how does it work? Well, people create a page for their project, describing what they want to do or make and explaining what help they need with it (in terms of books, if you're self-publishing, you may need to raise money to get the book edited and typeset, as well as paying for a cover designer to do a bespoke design). The projects that get the most views – and therefore, that raise the most money – are usually ones that have a video on their page, either showing what they plan to do, telling the story of their book in a fun, visual way, or simply showing a question and answer session with the person who's in charge. You can set a fundraising goal that you'd like to reach before the end of the project, and if you don't end up reaching that goal, no money is taken and you simply try your luck elsewhere. This prevents the possibility of you raising just some of the money, meaning that you wouldn't be able to complete the project and resulting in a lot of angry backers who wouldn't receive their rewards. You can crowdfund pretty much anything these days, but books and publishing is one area that has always received a lot of positive feedback. Just make sure that your book has a unique angle, something new and exciting that'll get people interested.

Looking at crowdfunding websites can generally be very inspiring as well – you'll see all these entrepreneurs out there, trying to get their book off the ground, or trying to create something truly unique, and it may well push you into getting on with your own project, whether you try and raise money for it or not. Seeing people putting themselves out there – baring their souls to try and complete a project – is pretty incredible, and seeing when people actually achieve their dreams (such as when I bought the book I'd backed) can have a really positive effect on your mindset. They can do it, and so can you. Invest in something, go on a journey with another author, and perhaps consider setting up your own fundraising page – just make sure you've got good stuff to offer your backers, otherwise no one's going to be interested in it.

Some popular crowdfunding websites (not necessarily focusing on publishing) include:

Kickstarter - www.kickstarter.com
Indiegogo - www.indiegogo.com

Rockethub - www.rockethub.com
GoGetFunding - gogetfunding.com
FundRazr - www.fundrazr.com
Crowdrise - www.crowdrise.com
GoFundMe - www.gofundme.com
Crowdfunder - www.crowdfunder.co.uk

These are also listed in the Resources section at the end of this book.

Making Your Author Website

You might not want to even think about making an author website until you've finished your first book, but it's probably one of the most important things you'll need to do as an author (a web presence of just a Facebook page and a Twitter profile isn't really going to cut it), and it can also be fun and – yes, you've guessed it – motivational! You can have a serious, corporate-looking website, or you can be a bit creative and have your website match your personality or your genre of books. After trying many different ways of making sites over the years, I now use Wix, and you can use this for free if you're just starting up. Once you begin to get traffic to the site, however, I recommend paying for the premium service (without the ads) to make your website look as professional as possible.

I didn't want a boring website, so I tried to use a similar theme to my Little Forest paranormal mystery series of novels. The main colours used are black, white and red, and the background is of a creepy forest, with my title banner also featuring one of the forest photos I used for my *Carnival Masquerade* book cover. I wanted everything about the site to reflect the types of books I write, and it was really fun putting it all together (and changing it every few months when I think of something new to add).

In terms of Wix, there are several options if you want to pay, and you can choose from monthly or annual payments. To give you an idea, the 'eCommerce' package (for small businesses) is £10.10 a month, the 'Unlimited' package (for entrepreneurs and freelancers – this is the package I have) is £7.76 a month, and the 'Combo' package (for personal use) is £5.16 a month, at the time of writing. Of course, there are a lot of other website builders and hosts out there, and WordPress is another popular one. Just remember that as well as a website, if you want to look professional, you'll have to pay for a domain name too (for example, mine is www.jessicagracecoleman.com). A lot of website builder and host sites will offer this service.

Making your own website can be fun, it is definitely a way of procrastiworking rather than procrastinating, and it can be a great motivator, so if you haven't started already, open up an account today! Here are a few website builders and hosts to choose from, and these are also listed in the Resources section in the appendix:

Wix - www.wix.com
WordPress - wordpress.com
GoDaddy - www.godaddy.com
1and1 - www.1and1.co.uk
Moonfruit - www.moonfruit.com
Ehost - www.ehost.com
HostClear - www.hostclear.com
Idea Host - www.ideahost.com
Weebly - www.weebly.com

Relax And Reset Your Brain

Sometimes – even if we have deadlines looming at us – we just need to sit back, relax, and reset our brains. If you work too hard (at anything in life) without taking enough breaks, you could risk 'burnout', which is not something you want to experience, as you won't be getting any work done then at all. There's only so much stressing you can do about a book before it starts to consume your every waking thought (and your dreams), so often the best thing you can do is just try and forget about it for a while. Easier said than done, I know, but here are some ideas to clear your mind, if only for a few minutes.

Bath, Wine And Music

These days, everyone's so busy and rushing around that we never seem to have the time to relax in our own homes, and I'm thinking in particular of our bathrooms. We have the quickest showers possible so we can get up and out to work, completely ignoring our lovely large baths (if you have one). It may be an oldie, but it's a goodie: run some water for a bath, add in some bubble bath and other luxurious toiletries, put some soothing music on, light a few candles, and – if you're so inclined – grab a nice glass of wine. Lie back, and relax. You know the saying about how a change can be just as good as a holiday? Well, if you don't usually have them, make the effort to have a long, comforting bath every so often, and use that time to shut off your mind as much as you can. Listen to the music, feel the warmth of the water against your skin, and relax your entire body.

People generally don't take enough time to relax these days, and when it can be as simple as running a bath, why not at least give it a try? If turning your brain off isn't the problem, you can also use this relaxing bath time to run through storylines and dialogue in your head; the change from being at your desk to being in a lovely bath could help you look at your plot and characters from a different perspective. Either way, you can't really say anything bad about a nice, relaxing bath.

Meditation

Like with the mantras in the self-belief section, this won't be for everyone, by hey – if you don't try, you'll never know, will you? If you have a lot going on in your life (work, family, social life, hobbies, and trying to fit writing around all of it), it can be far too easy to become exhausted and irritated, and if this is the case, you're probably not going to find the time to sit down and get that novel written. One way of getting around this is to set aside a few minutes every day to sit and meditate. This doesn't necessarily mean sitting in a yoga pose and going 'Ommmm' (although you can do if you want); it basically means finding somewhere quiet to sit down and spend a few moments alone, clearing your brain of all your worries and just 'being' in the moment.

If you like, do it once in the morning and once in the evening, to reset your mind and focus on you and your body, on your breathing and your posture as you sit and 'get away from it all'. If you do this before your writing sessions, your brain will get used to the 'meditation followed by work' part of your routine, and you may find that 'resetting' your brain through meditation works wonders for your concentration in those few hours or minutes when you get to write.

Clear Your Mind Through Activity

You may be thinking that the last thing you need to do is to clear your mind when you're trying to come up with the answer to a complex plot question, or when you're trying to decide what your baddie would do next, but sometimes we just have to stop our brains for a moment and focus on something else. This comes into play when you go for a walk, getting some fresh air and 'clearing your head' as you focus on putting one leg in front of the other. Some of our best thinking is done when we're trying *not* to think, but if you just sit on your sofa and try not to think about your book, the first thing you'll start thinking about is – that's right – your book.

So what else can you do? Some people like to drive, and not just when they're going through a creative block – they drive to clear their mind of all thoughts, especially if something's going wrong in their life. Just get on the open road and see where you end up... something which I think would always be best in the summer in some kind of automatic convertible on one of those nice, long, straight roads in America. Driving in a clapped out manual banger through the chaotic streets of London, for example, may not have the same effect.

Driving is also good for when you're thinking about possible plot lines, but obviously it's important to keep your main concentration on the road! Because of this – and bear with me, I know it's a little strange – I suggest fake driving: driving on a computer game. Games that involve cars to travel around the virtual city may not have driving aimlessly as their main objective, but it can be a pretty good alternative if you find that driving helps you think. Plus, it doesn't matter in games if you accidentally crash into someone else's car when you get an amazing plot idea, or if you mistakenly drive into the sea when your brain suddenly gives you a brilliant way of filling in that annoying plot hole that's been plaguing you for months. If you're an obsessive gamer, this may not be the best idea, as gaming is likely to overtake your good intentions of creative thinking and you'll come to your senses after several hours, with no plot issues sorted out but a whole load of points racked up in your virtual world.

Some people prefer to move while they think, either through doing the customary 'walk in the fresh air' or by doing some proper, full-on exercise. Go for a run or to the gym, and while those lovely endorphins are running through your body, why not run through your novel's plot in your head? Or just let your mind wander and see if that plot hole will fill itself in – I'm amazed by how many times I've done this while not thinking about anything in particular. Your brain is a clever little sausage and keeps whirring away even when you think it's not doing anything. I've even worked out plot holes in my dreams before (the idea is usually surrounded by a whole host of crazy goings on that have nothing to do with my work – or apparently with anything – but it has happened). If you're that passionate about your writing, if you're really into your novel and determined to get your story sorted, your brain will magically continue to work through it even when you're otherwise occupied.

Getting back to the exercise thing, I turned my garage into a mini gym, so if I'm stuck on something plot-wise or just feel like I need to get some inspiration (or time away from the computer or the TV or the millions of other screens we seemingly deal with on a daily basis), I pop into the gym for an hour or so. I turn on some cheesy music (usually some pop punk from my teenage years that I know off by heart), and get exercising. Even if I don't solve any of my writing problems, it's a good break, and it gives me an extra energy boost to carry on with my writing. And hitting a punch bag is a really good way to get rid of any writing (or other) frustrations!

Holiday

Of course, the whole 'change is as good as a holiday' thing works just as well if you actually have a holiday. If you've been trying to write that novel all year, every day, and have come to a complete halt with it, going away for your summer holiday could be the break your brain needs to reset itself, and when you come back, you may find that you can sit down and write as if there were never any problems. Often it can be the week or two away from a computer screen as much as anything else, or you may have more time to read on holiday and rediscover why you love books so much, spurring you on to write your own.

You may even find that you start to miss sitting down every day and trying to write, reigniting your passion ready for when you get back home. And let me tell you, a spurt of activity after a week or two away from your normal life can really help when it comes to the post-holiday blues. You'll also feel like you got much more for your money than what you paid for the holiday – you also got your mojo back. If you haven't got any holidays planned or can't afford one, how about a mini-break in your own country? A long weekend in a different city or by the sea can work wonders, or perhaps even just a daytrip to a local spa to get pampered. Reset your body, reset your brain, and get back to writing.

Travel

OK, so not everyone has the time or money to go travelling in order to gain experiences and see life from a different perspective, but if you do, this can be a brilliant way to expand your horizons and fill your head with ideas for stories. I've been fortunate enough to travel to some brilliant faraway places, but I've also got just as many ideas from visiting different towns, villages and cities in my own country (England, in case you hadn't guessed). This is part of the whole 'write what you know' thing, and I would never have thought of the ideas for some of my stories if I hadn't visited wonderful places myself. For instance, *The Park* from my short story collection, *Grown By The Wicked Moon*, is based on Buddha Park in Vientiane, Laos. I was overwhelmed by the size and scope of the statues that make up Buddha Park, and even as I was wandering around the surreal landscape, I was creating a story in my mind. If I hadn't visited there, I wouldn't have even known it had existed, and I never would have wrote that story.

Travel From The Comfort Of Your Own Home

Of course, in this day and age there are endless ways around the whole travelling thing. The Internet is a wonderful resource (not to mention brilliant procrastination tool, or 'procrastiworking' tool!), and if you want to, you can travel around the entire world from the comfort of your living room. Use Google Images or Google Maps for a quick snapshot of places, YouTube videos from travellers who've recorded their own experiences, catch up TV to watch some beautifully shot documentaries from hundreds of different countries, and movies that were shot in amazing locations – all of these things can help inspire you. Film and TV can be utilised in so many different ways, and inspiration for locations in your book is just one of them.

Go For A Walk

Travel doesn't necessarily mean getting on a train or a plane; it can also mean simply going for a walk, getting away from your computer and being outside. Take in the scenery, watch people interacting, and see what words come to mind as you go. Type notes in your phone or talk into a dictation app or voice recorder (such as Voice Record Pro or Smart Voice Recorder), then when you're back home, you can refer back to anything that inspired you during your trek.

So, where should you go for your walk? It depends where you live, of course, but I always find getting back to nature really helps when I'm trying to think of plot lines (and how to fill in those pesky plot holes). I'm lucky enough to live near the beautiful Cannock Chase, an area of outstanding natural beauty that I used to model the Great Specton Woods on in my Little Forest series. A walk through here, especially when it's getting on for autumn and winter and is a little gloomy and a little desolate, really gets me in the right head space to write about all the spooky goings on in the woods in my series. In this case, the setting matches the setting in my books, which is always helpful, and this can work with other places too.

Are you writing about a group of friends who live in the city? Why not go for a night out in a similar city, or gather your friends together and have a day exploring the sights? If your book is set in a small rural community, try going for a walk around fields and farms, breathing in the fresh country air and letting those storylines start to form in the back of your mind. Take in everything around you – the sights, the smells, the sounds – as these will really help when you come to set the scene in your book. Take notes as you go, and photos can be a great way to recall things your memory may have forgotten by the time you get back and sit down at your computer. Of course, this technique won't work for everyone – you can't easily go for a walk in New York City if you're in a little village in the North of England, and I wouldn't recommend roaming around anywhere at night to in order to get into the mindset of your crazed antagonist, but it's a starting point, at least.

Here are some of the apps mentioned in this section (also listed on the Resources page):

Google Images - images.google.com
Google Maps - maps.google.co.uk
YouTube - www.youtube.com
Voice Record Pro -
www.bejbej.info/app/voicerecordpro

Literary Tourism

There's also something called Literary Tourism, which I love, and which I'd like to do a lot more of. If I'm visiting somewhere for fun and I see a tourist attraction regarding a writer or a place where a writer lived, I usually have to go and see it. I went to see a gig in London one weekend and when I realised my hotel was close to the Charles Dickens Museum, I made sure I squeezed in a little visit. The same happened when I was travelling in the US and found myself in Baltimore, Maryland – it may be a bit morbid, but as a fan of Edgar Allan Poe, I made sure I went to see his grave, which is a pretty big tourist attraction to writers, and as you'd expect, has many strange stories surrounding it (such as the mysterious visitor who used to leave roses and cognac at his grave on the anniversary of the author's death). I'm also fortunate enough to live not too far away from Shakespeare's Birthplace, Stratford-upon-Avon, and every time I visit there, I'm filled with inspiration and motivation to get going on my own work. If you visit, it's lovely in the summer (if you can put up with the tourists), or if you go on Shakespeare's birthday in April, they usually have a parade and all kinds of celebrations.

Literary Tourism can include visiting places where famous authors were born, where they lived, where they died, and where they're now buried, but it can also mean visiting places they were inspired by, travelling the route of one of your favourite characters, or visiting locations where movies and TV versions were filmed. There are also the guided tours based on literary figures, or you can make your own pilgrimage to places that mean something to you literature-wise. There's a lot of different and fun stuff you can do.

So, next time you're on holiday, see if there's anywhere literary-related where you can pop in and visit to get that inspiration flowing. I find that just being in the same places that famous writers once inhabited – and being reminded of all their great work – is a brilliant motivator, and it may get you thinking about your own stories and what you want to achieve as a writer yourself. If you have the time, the money, and the inclination, you could even plan a road trip to visit several of these literary landmarks, and why not keep a diary as you go to keep your own writing going while you're away from your computer? Who knows – there could be a book in it.

You can find a list of literary tourist hotspots in the appendix of this book, in the Literary Tourism Travel Plan section.

Writing Retreats

You've probably heard of writing retreats, and you probably have quite a good idea of what they entail. I know that before I went on, I pictured a retreat much like a scene from a period drama, with the author (who for some reason was wearing a long, Victorian style dress and bonnet) sitting in a lovely English country garden, drinking tea while writing in a leather-bound journal with a delicate fountain pen, or perhaps a quill. As it turned out, the one I went on wasn't dissimilar, although I definitely wasn't wearing a dress and bonnet and I had my trusty laptop instead of a book and quill.

There are many different types of writing retreats you can go on, all around the world, but I chose mine for several reasons: it was based in the Forest of Dean – somewhere I'd never been but had wanted to see – it was run by a lovely vegetarian lady who offered home cooked food three times a day as part of the package, and it was really good value for money. If you're interested, the lady's name is Annie McKie and her website is listed at the end of this section and on the Resources page of the appendix.

So, I booked my five days away a couple of months in advance, and when the day came, I loaded my car with my stuff and drove for two and a half hours to my destination. It was a lovely part of the country, and from the hamlet where the house was situated (in a valley), you had a wonderful view of the surrounding forest. You were cut off from civilisation here (my car – which is tiny – could only just squeeze through the incredibly narrow roads to get to the house), and that is exactly what I wanted. I was greeted at the gate by the woman who ran the retreat and her beautiful lurcher dog, and then I was taken to my room – which was more like a mini suite – in an annex off the side of their house. I had a bed, a log burner, my own bathroom, and my own access to the balcony that looked out over the Forest of Dean – a spectacular view, especially when the sun was just coming up.

It depends on the retreat you go on, of course, but with mine I was left to my own devices most of the time. My first and last evenings were spent eating with the lady and her husband downstairs in the main house, but other than that my meals were brought to me (placed just outside my room so I wouldn't be disturbed) morning, noon and night. As a vegetarian myself, I always looked forward to these meals, and they were always absolutely delicious and laid out beautifully. Everything seemed to be home grown or organic, with honey from the community's bees and eggs from the community's chickens, and the homemade desserts were amazing.

It was a great place to write. I would get up in the morning, have my breakfast, then start on my work until lunch, when I'd again have a great meal (I must have put weight on during those five days, but it was worth it). Then (unless I was in the zone), I could go for a walk in the forest, one part of which was just a two minute walk from the house. I was told to look out for the wild boars but I didn't see any, which I was more than a little thankful for – the last thing I needed was to be out walking in the fresh country air, getting inspiration, only to be chased until I fell over! I would then work until dinnertime, when I'd again eat far too much. After dinner I would read (something that I don't get as much time to do as I'd like) and then head to bed. In those five days I got the whole of my novel plotted out and 25,000 words written.

Getting away from your daily life is really good for focusing your mind, not to mention the fact that you know you're paying to be there; if you left at the end of your stay having written nothing, you'd feel like a bit of an idiot. I toyed with not connecting to the Internet for those five days, as I'm sure you know all about the procrastination potential of the web, but in the end I did connect. My business was in its early months at that point and I wanted to keep on top of my emails, and I also didn't want to disconnect myself from the world too much – for some reason, I work better when I know there's the possibility to take a break and check out how people are doing online. I didn't use it much, though, and I spent my time there doing one of five main things: writing, reading, walking in the forest, eating, and sleeping. It was pretty great.

Included in my stay was a mind mapping session with the woman who ran it. She was also a writer and I talked through my plot with her, telling her my problems and plot holes and coming up with ideas to try and fix them. She had some great ideas, and she recommended a couple of books to me (that she then leant me). That and the discussions at my two dinners in the house really inspired me and gave me some brilliant ideas to work with. The whole thing was a great success, and I plan on going back when I can.

There are hundreds of retreats out there, all in different locations and with different focuses. I've toyed with going on a retreat abroad, somewhere like France maybe – I once saw one based in a French Chateau that I thought looked pretty poetic – but there are many different countries you can go to. You can attend one similar to the retreat I went on, where it's just you on your own (the only writer at the retreat), or you can go on one where there's a group of writers, where you each do your own thing in the day and then meet up for the evening meal, chatting about literature and your own projects while secretly sizing each other up (I'm sure that doesn't happen – not everywhere, at least). Think of *Tamara Drewe*, if you've seen it, but without Gemma Arterton wandering around the place in tiny denim shorts.

Then there are the retreats that involve actual classes, presentations, workshops and discussions – these are obviously ones to go on if you're more interested in learning about the craft than just getting on with your own project. I went on my retreat to give myself the time (and permission) to start getting those words on the page, and while away from my usual environment and all the things that usually indicated to me that I should be working or doing something else, I found that the words just flowed out of me. If I'd been stopping every few hours to attend workshops, I wouldn't have got in the zone. Quite often I write best when I know I don't have to stop at a certain time – like if I have the whole evening to work on my own project or if I've taken a day off and don't have any other plans that will interrupt me being in the zone.

I didn't have any interruptions at my writer's retreat except for the food three times a day, and that was a brilliant interruption. It allowed me to take a break from my computer screen, sit in a different place in the room, put on some music, and really enjoy the food. One thing that helped when I was at my retreat was that there was no TV in the room and the Internet signal I could get on my computer wasn't fast enough to stream anything. Goodbye procrastination in the form of TV, Netflix, Amazon Instant Video and YouTube. There was a radio in the room and a bookshelf full of books, but apart from that, it was just me and the writing.

I've also considered giving myself a bit of a 'DIY' writer's retreat, and this would suit people who really can't get on with their work unless they have zero distractions. If you can afford it, book a hotel room for a few nights, in a different part of the country, but not somewhere that's surrounded by a lot of shops or things to do. Get away from your life, check in, and get to work. It always helps to make sure there's a desk in the room before you book, or at least a nice comfy chair you can sit in while balancing your laptop on your knees. Of course, even with hotel rooms you still get distractions – such as housekeeping and other guests constantly arriving and leaving – but hopefully there will be fewer distractions than you're used to.

If you're looking to stay in a more unique place (and often for less money), I'd recommend Air B&B. I've used it in the past when going on holidays, and the variety of places you can find on there is amazing. These are generally people's homes, and they rent out their entire place while they themselves are off travelling, or they simply rent out rooms in their houses if you'd prefer a bit of company when hanging out in the shared areas. Sometimes the rooms to stay in are annexes on people's homes, so you can have your space but there is also someone nearby if you have any problems. Whatever you choose, you can quite often end up spending less money than you would for a hotel room, and you can end up staying in an entire house or apartment. I've always thought many places on Air B&B would make for great writer's retreats, especially as they're available not just all over the country but all over the world. You could even do a writer's retreat tour, staying in several different places, writing by day and exploring the area by night (or vice versa).

It can be a particularly good idea to go and stay in a similar place to the locations in your novels. If you live in a city but are writing about the countryside, rent a place out in the sticks to get into the right mindset. It was great when I was in the Forest of Dean, as a lot of the themes in the novel I was working on were to do with nature and the earth, so wandering around the woods was great for getting in the right mood. Whatever you do, you'll hopefully find that leaving your normal surroundings with the express intent to get some writing done will motivate you to actually do it, especially as you'll be paying for the privilege and will want something to show for it.

Here are a few links to Writer's Retreats in England and beyond (they are also listed in the Resources section at the end of the book):

The Watermill, Italy - www.watermill.net
Moniack Mhor, Scotland - www.moniackmhor.org.uk
Urban Writers' Retreat, Devon - http://www.urbanwritersretreat.co.uk/a-residential-writing-retreat/
Annie McKie Retreats, Writing and Communication Services - www.anniemckie.co.uk
The Grange, short breaks by the sea - www.thegrangebythesea.com

The Meanings Of Names

Names. Names are incredibly important, whether we're talking characters, locations, or even pen names. Let's focus now, however, on the names we give our characters. I find that if I'm having trouble coming up with characters for my stories, I start with their names. Of course, not all characters' names will mean something or relate to their personality (how often does that happen in real life?!) but you can definitely have some fun with names. This can be an enjoyable, easy part of planning your novel, but sometimes (when brain fried, for example) you may need a little help. Here are my favourite ways of coming up with character names.

First of all, see if you can give some of your characters names that mean something in relation to who they are, or where they live, or what they do. It doesn't have to be anything ridiculously obvious (like Samuel Baker, the baker, or Dennis Butcher, the butcher) but you can put subtle hints into your characters' names that give clues to the reader about what may be coming. This is often easier to do with surnames rather than first names, and it can often depend on what genre you're writing in, but why not give it a go? If you're stuck in the planning stage of your novel, creating fun and interesting names for your characters can really help – it'll allow you to picture your characters more clearly, and as the world of your novel starts to take shape, you'll want to dive in and get writing as quickly as you can.

There are quite a few fun websites and apps you can use when coming up with character names, and even if you don't use the actual names they come up with (after all, other writers could be using these apps as well!) they can give you some good ideas. More on this in a bit.

Baby Name Websites

There are hundreds of websites that list names, for several different purposes, and baby names can be a good place to start, as these are often split into girls and boys and are also listed alphabetically. If you have a favourite name or names chosen for your future children, however, I'd steer clear from using them – the last thing you want is for your child to be named after a famous character when your books inevitably become best sellers (especially if you've used their name for the antagonist in your story)! Some sites list popular baby names by the year, which is really useful if you're writing about a past decade. Websites for this include:

BabyNames.co.uk
The Guardian – 100 Most Popular Baby Names 2014 - www.theguardian.com/news/datablog/ng-interactive/2015/aug/17/100-most-popular-baby-names-england-wales-full-list
BabyNames.com
BabyNames.org.uk
Baby Center – Popular Baby Names For US By Year -

www.babycenter.com

These are also listed in the Resources section of the appendix.

Geographical/Historical Name Websites

These are brilliant sources of information if you're writing about a certain time period, or about another country whose popular names you may not be as familiar with. You can get these listed by first and last names, and often the sites will give you information regarding the origin of a name, so you can really put some thought into the background of your characters, naming them after their personalities (which I think is nice to do even if your readers may not ever realise the reasons for their names).

These sites are good for choosing names, yes, but they're also quite inspirational. If you're not sure about any of your characters yet, spend some time browsing through names – something might leap out at you, and you might start getting weird and wonderful ideas. This particularly works for fantasy and historical books, where the names can be bizarrely beautiful – think *Lord Of The Rings*, for example. Websites for this include:

Behind The Name – History Names -
www.behindthename.com/names/usage/history
Behind The Name – English Surnames -
surnames.behindthename.com/names/usage/english
Name Nerds – Irish Names - www.namenerds.com/irish
European Baby Names And Meanings -
babynames.allparenting.com/babynames/Tips/European
_Baby_Names_and_Meanings/

<u>Popular Norse Names</u> - babynames.net/all/old-norse

These are also listed in the Resources section of the appendix.

Apps

There are several apps that are cheap (or free), fun, and may give you a little boost when you're trying to think of names (or, indeed, characters and their traits). 'Name Dice' is a random name generator, with the first name appearing on a picture of one die and the last name appearing on the other. It's very much like picking out random names for your Sims, and while there are some slightly rarer names in there, it's mainly modern ones (so no ye olde fantasy names). For example, on my first three goes of 'throwing' the dice, I got 'Quinn Parks', 'Kira Blake' and 'Billy Brady'. I quite like Kira Blake, actually… this is available from the Apple app store and for android, and it's absolutely free. As an aside, the same people (Thinkamingo) also have a 'Story Dice' app, although it is aimed at perhaps younger people – it works on the same principle, but throws out dice with pictures on the side to get you thinking. For example: an aeroplane, a man on a parachute, and a pair of scissors. Like I said, it seems like it's for kids, but when you're stuck in the land of the dreaded creative block, sometimes it's the simple things that will help get you out of it! This one you do have to pay for, however, and at the time of writing it costs £1.49. You can also get a 'Creative Writing Bundle' from Thinkamingo for £5.99 that includes Story Dice, Story Park, Lists for Writers and Spooky Story Dice (the latter definitely looks as if it's meant for kids, but again, that doesn't mean you can't enjoy it too!)

In my own books, names can mean different things, whether they're of people or places. My main character, for example, is called Beth Powers, a not-so-subtle hint that Beth may well start gaining powers of her own in the future. Most of the rest of the names used in the Little Forest series were chosen in order to give an overall feeling of small village, country living. We have Max Rivers, Daniel Fields, and Rick Wood to evoke images of the countryside, not to mention Mrs Teasdale and Reverend Kipling, my homage to tea and cake – something that is quintessentially British. I also did a similar thing with place names. The stately home that holds the eerie, 'chilling' Hallowe'en celebrations is called Chillingsley Hall, while the town of Willowton yet again invokes images of trees and forests. The village of Renfield is a slight homage to the 'crazy' character in Dracula, as sanity and insanity are big themes in the series, and then we have the county of Covershire, so named because of the images of covertness and maybe even covens that it evokes – hinting at the magical elements of the series.

Start thinking about the themes and ideas you're exploring in your novel or story. Can you reflect any of these notions in the names of your characters or places? This can be a fun exercise, but make sure you don't get caught up in it too much! Some characters with normal sounding names will help ground your book in reality – if that's what you want, of course. Place names can be fun as well, and in general I find the idea of world building one of the best things about writing a novel (obviously you don't need to do any major world building if you're setting your story in an existing place). There is more on world building elsewhere in these books, and also in the appendix.

Creative Ways To Start Creative Writing

Volume Three

by

Jessica Grace Coleman

Music

I find music to be a huge help when both planning and writing my novels, and because of this it is mentioned in several places in these books. Music can help you get into the creative zone when you're sitting down to write, but it can also help in other ways – especially if you're away from your computer and have time to think about your work in a different way.

Music To Inspire

While I was travelling in Asia, I was in the middle of writing my first novel in the Little Forest series, *The Former World*, and during the long hours of travelling on coaches, minibuses, boats, taxis and planes, I started coming up with ways to get into the creative mood. I didn't have time to really get into any proper writing in between visiting all these amazing places, and I couldn't always make notes on my phone or my travel diary as I tend to suffer from travel sickness if I concentrate too hard on any one object, but what I could do was listen to music.

So, I spent those long hours staring out the window of

whatever form of transport I was in and listening to music on my phone. The mixture of the beautiful scenery (we spent most of two days travelling through Laos on a mini bus, the fog that surrounded the mountains looking like something out of *Jurassic Park*) and the music was pretty inspirational in itself, but I found myself creating playlists of songs and tracks that would accompany my novel. I started with my main character, choosing the kind of pop punk songs she'd listen to, then changed to one of the other characters, and the darker, rockier type of songs he'd listen to, and so on. I also had a playlist for the two main characters (who were best friends) with songs that illustrated their particular relationship. It was a fun exercise to do, and it really helped me get into the minds of my characters at a time when I couldn't actually carry on writing my novel. I also made (very quick) notes on my phone whenever a scene or backstory idea came to me, and most of these ideas came out of the very songs themselves.

Using Playlists

Some writers create playlists for all of their books, listening to them as they plan and then write the actual novel. Personally, I've always had issues listening to music while I type, as I inevitably get lost with what I'm doing and start typing out song lyrics in the middle of my sentences! Because of this, I usually have to work in silence, but sometimes silence is just too… well, silent, and that's when I turn to trusty Spotify. This is a great app for listening to music of all kinds, but it's also really useful for the playlists and 'compilations' they let you follow. I use the 'genres & moods' list when I'm writing, especially the 'focus' and 'chill' categories, which really – unsurprisingly – help you to focus and chill. I pay for the premium version of Spotify, which is around £10 a month, and it's worth it for not having to listen to all the ads. There are also some pretty interesting playlists, from 'Dinnertime Acoustics' to 'The Moon Is Calling' and 'Lost In the Woods' (that last one would fit pretty well with my series, actually). Finding music and playlists on YouTube works too, just make sure you don't spend all your time singing along to the songs instead of getting any work done! You can find lists of helpful playlists in the appendix.

Make The Most Of The Genre

Particular music genres, as well, can be very useful. Are you writing about a sweet country girl from Alabama or Indiana but have never visited America? Pop on an American Country playlist and really get in the mood. Writing about mods and rockers in 1950s Britain? Put on a playlist of music from that decade and country. Writing a drama set hundreds of years ago? Check out a Classical playlist. Getting into the mood of the time and place you're writing about can really help you get un-blocked, even if it's just a few words while you listen to the popular music from that place/era.

Music is incredibly useful when it comes to being creative and getting writing. You can use it to help you concentrate (especially if there are other noises in and outside your house that you want to drown out), you can use it to motivate yourself to get something done, and you can use it to soothe and relax you when you need a break from that screen.

Using Music For Scenes/Locations

As I've mentioned, another way you can use music is by creating playlists for your characters, and you can even create playlists scene by scene to help you picture what's happening. Here are some examples of the kinds of music that would be used in my Little Forest series, for some of my characters and for some of the scenes:

At the Stars and Stripes Diner – 50s/60s music. A Beach Boys song is mentioned in one scene.
At The Pit nightclub – rocky/alternative music.
Scenes with the band Random Violation – upbeat, pop punk type tracks.
Scenes in the traditional Irish pubs in Ireland in *The Gloaming* – old country folk songs.
Frightfest taking place at Chillingsley Hall stately home – classical music, with a hint of creepiness for Hallowe'en.
The fireworks scene at Little Forest Castle in *The Former World* – 'The Greatest View' by Silverchair. I was thinking of a fireworks display I'd attended myself where that song was played during the finale.
The song 'Jerusalem' is a big part of the plot of *The Former World*.
The Gloaming is based on (and makes use of) the song 'Roamin' in the Gloamin'' by Harry Lauder.
The carnival (Doctor Blackout's Magnificent Masquerade Carnival) in *Carnival Masquerade* would be full of creepy, old-fashioned carnival music, mentioned in the book. It was what I was thinking of when I wrote some of those scenes.
In *The Exalted* we learn about Beatrice Rosier's past in the 1920s – I was thinking of lavish parties and 'hot' jazz music for this.

When you start thinking about it, music links really well with literature, so why not try making your own playlists?

I've listed some Spotify categories in the appendix in the 'Creative Playlists' section. Here you'll get some ideas for relaxation, motivation, concentration, and travel playlists (the latter go hand in hand with the Literary Tourism section).

Get Crafty

Computers, websites and apps aren't for everyone. If you have a day job that involves sitting at a computer for eight hours and feeling your eyes going square at the screen, you're unlikely to want to spend any more of your free time on the computer than you absolutely have to (and you probably will have to in order to write your book, unless you're doing it really old style with a typewriter or a quill and ink). So, what does this leave us with? Crafts!

I'm not saying you need to knit a tea cosy or suddenly start tie-dying everything to within an inch of its life, but sometimes getting away from the computer and using your hands for something really creative can get you in the right mindset. These can include crafts not related to your work at all – if you know how to knit, for instance, you can think of plot lines and dialogue while fashioning a lovely winter scarf – or they can be directly linked to your writing work, like with the following examples.

Make A Collage

One way to do this is to start collaging. Grab a magazine and pick out someone who resembles your main character, then pick out some outfits they'd wear, and the kinds of CDs and DVDs they'd be into (or downloads and streamed movies, if you want to be all modern about it). Look up locations online and print out pictures to put in a scrapbook. If you can draw, draw your characters or your locations, scribble their interests in different colour pens, illustrate their dreams and desires. There are all kinds of things you can do, and if you put all of this into one book, you can open it whenever you want and get inspired to carry on with your novel.

The scrapbook can also be useful to refer back to if you can't remember something about a character's personality, or their date of birth or the colour of their eyes. I did this for my first novel, and it featured things such as character profiles, a map of the main village where the series was set, events from the main character's past that could turn up in one of the books, a list of secondary characters, a list of locations, a timeline for things that happened to the main characters both before and during the book, song names and lyrics for my fictional band, Random Violation, vague work/shift timetables for the main characters, and much more. Creating this book helped me get into the mindset of the characters, it gave me more of a feel for the location of Little Forest, and it got my ever-tired eyes away from a bright computer screen to boot.

Getting Artistic With Drawings

If you're talented when it comes to drawing, why not put that to use when you're planning your novel?

Personally, I'm awful at drawing, and sketching my main characters did not go down well at all, but if these are going to be for your eyes only, what does it matter? (Unless, of course, you get really famous and someone finds one of your character sketches lying around – so if they're bad, maybe think about burning them afterwards!)

So yes, drawing. When planning your novel, if the words aren't coming, maybe the pictures will. Why not fill a sketchbook with drawings of your main characters, drawings of locations and settings used in the books (and maps), and even drawings of particular scenes in your book? It's all about immersing yourself in that world even before you start writing, and sketches can be a great way of doing this.

Of course, if you're not talented in the drawing stakes, there are always other things you can do (like collaging from online images and sticking in photos you've printed out from your own camera). Then, whenever you get stuck with your writing, you can flick through the scrapbook or sketchbook and hopefully get your mojo back. If nothing else, it will tell you that at one point you put a lot of time, energy and effort into planning this book (even down to cutting out pictures and sticking them to a page, or drawing people who may or may not look like actual people), and you don't want to let your past self down, do you? While you're at it, think again of your future self – all smug and sitting at their writing desk as they get to work on their fifth, or tenth, or twentieth novel – you don't want to disappoint them, do you?

Of course, you may be sick of thinking about your book,

in which case the last thing you want to do is attempt a character sketch of your main character or the house they live in. So, you can also use drawing to get into the zone by thinking about other books and your favourite characters in literature. Pick one of your favourite protagonists (or antagonists, I'm not judging) and draw them. Try and convey in your drawing what you feel about them, and how you picture them yourself (if different from a portrayal in a film/TV adaptation).

You can do the same with locations. For example, why not draw how you envisioned the desolate moors when reading *Wuthering Heights*? Again, if you don't have much talent for drawing, why not list your favourite characters (from literature, TV or film) and write down what it is about them that you like so much? You can do the same with locations from books, TV or film, as well as famous scenes, and again, you can make a collage or perhaps a Pinterest board to keep you inspired when writing your own novel. If you're more into cartoons, try converting one of your scenes into a comic (it doesn't have to be anything long or complicated – for instance, try a basic three-panel comic strip to get started). Actually, this can be a fun thing to do even if you're not stuck with your writing!

These exercises will get you thinking about your favourite books and characters in literature, and hopefully they'll stir something in you to get going on your own book.

Adult Colouring Books

These books have become very popular recently, and they're a great way of reawakening that creative mind within – and it's much easier than writing so there are no excuses! You don't have to have any particular artistic talent, just some pencils or pens and something to colour in. There are some brilliant books available to buy online, and all of the following can be bought from Amazon for between £4 - £8. The useful thing with Amazon listings is that you can 'look inside' to see the first few designs and decide whether or not they're right for you, but who doesn't like an exotic elephant or an octopus with tentacles just waiting to be made into art?! It's a great way of getting you in the zone, and with 'art therapy' being really big right now, it may help you relax and unwind from other areas of your life as well.

Here are some books you can try:

Millie Marotta's Animal Kingdom – A Colouring Book Adventure by Millie Marotta
Secret Garden: An Inky Treasure Hunt and Colouring Book by Johanna Basford
The Mindfulness Colouring Book: Anti-stress art therapy for busy people by Emma Farrarons
The Art Therapy Colouring Book by Richard Merritt and Hannah Davies
The Can't Sleep Colouring Book (Creative Colouring for Grown-Ups) by Various
Colour Therapy (Creative Colouring for Grown-Ups) by Cindy Wilde and Laura-Kate Chapman
Japanese Patterns (Creative Colouring for Grown-Ups) by Various Authors

All of these titles are also listed in the Resources section in the appendix.

If you don't want to buy an entire book, you can

download some of these images online to 'try before your buy'. It won't be for everyone, but it's a great way of acting like a child while pretending you're actually an adult, and it can do the trick of resetting your brain in its creative zone, preparing you for your next writing session.

Scribble

If a blank document on a screen is too daunting, start by taking out a notepad and get doodling. Sketch some of your characters, draw one of the locations, or just scribble out words you think you might want to use. Scribble sentences. Scribble names. No matter what you do, just keep scribbling. Many of us succumb to mindless doodling during the workday, but you can take that mindless scribbling and turn it into scribbling of value. Just scribble anything you can think of to get your ideas down on paper. If it works, you can type any useful word scribblings up later when you're not feeling so daunted by the whole thing.

If you're not much of a pen and paper type person, there are also several websites and apps you can use to the same effect. I find these often work best on tablets as it's still allowing you to get away from that computer and that blank document, even if you want to stick with using a screen. Noteshelf is an app that will allow you to take notes, or try Fifty Three or Moleskine journal. Use your fingertips or a stylus and just let those ideas flow out!

Noteshelf - www.noteshelf.net
Fifty Three - www.fiftythree.com
Moleskine Journal -

www.moleskine.com/microsites/apps

These are also listed in the Resources section of the appendix.

Being Crafty Online

If after your crafty break you are willing to get back on the computer, there are crafty things you can do online as well. For example, pin images to some boards on Pinterest – you can create a board for locations, a board for clothes your main character would wear, places they'd hang out, books they'd read, and so on. Create a personality board for each character, and then, if you want to stick with the old skool way of doing things, print them out and put them in a scrapbook. Some people work better with visuals than with words, so this can really help when you're getting ready to start that book.

There are ways of creating virtual scrapbooks if you prefer this method, although it might be an idea to do this on a tablet or something away from the usual computer you write with, just to separate it all out a bit more.

Making Use Of Films And The Theatre

Literature, films and theatre are all very much interlinked, so it's strange to think how many writers don't consider these other forms of media when writing their novels. Of course, this won't apply to everyone, but here are some little exercises and ideas concerning film, TV and plays that may help you in your writing quest:

Get To Grips With Plays

Even if you have no interest whatsoever in being a playwright, it can be a really eye-opening exercise to read a play and then go and see it performed. Take Shakespeare, for example. Especially over summer, it seems like you can't go anywhere without seeing a production of a Shakespeare play being advertised – my town does one every year outside the Castle, something which inspired one of my scenes in *The Former World* during the Hallowe'en Fright Fest celebrations. Shakespeare's plays are readily available online and as free ebook collections, so it's easier than ever before to read them without spending any money. Why not read the play and then go and see it in action? See how the actors portray the characters? See if any lines of dialogue jump out at you that you totally missed when reading it? See how it comes to life in front of you, and see how the dialogue is interpreted by those performing it. Thinking about these kinds of things can help you when it comes to your own writing (even if you're not writing a play or anything like it), and personally, seeing a live production always inspires me to go home and write.

While you're at it, if you've enjoyed watching plays, why not get involved with a local theatre group or kid's theatre group and see if you can offer your writing services? On the other hand, just volunteer and see how they work – witness how the story gets from the page onto the stage. It could get you thinking about your own work, and it might even inspire you to get involved with the theatre on a more permanent basis.

Watch Some Good TV And Films

Moving on from plays, it can also be a useful exercise to study scripts for films and TV shows (again, even if you're not planning on being a screenwriter), and with so many great TV shows being made recently, you're spoiled for choice. Either before or after you watch your chosen film or TV program, take a look at the script and see not only how it was written, but how it was transferred to the screen. Did the actors deliver the dialogue in the same way as you did in your head when you read the words in the screenplay? Was the action as you expected or had it changed? What about the structure of the story and how it concluded? Thinking about these things in terms of TV shows and films can be just as useful when it comes to storytelling as thinking about dialogue and scenes in books. Plus, this way, if anyone asks, you can say that you're not just being lazy by watching these films and TV shows but are actually procrastiworking. See, being a writer rocks!

A good exercise when talking about screenwriting and plays is to take a part of your novel and write it as if it were a scene in a play or a film. It gets you looking at your work from a different perspective, and you may see things you missed when you were focusing on getting exactly the right words in your prose. It can be a fun activity to do, and it might even get you interested in screenwriting!

Become An Actor Yourself

As well as being a brilliant writer, Charles Dickens was extremely fond of the theatre and of performing, and as well as directing some plays, he would also travel around and give readings or small performances of scenes from his books. Now, I'm not saying you start randomly standing up in book shops and reading from your soon-to-be-published novel, but public readings and performances are some of the ways you can get excited about writing again (if you're of a theatrical, dramatic persuasion anyway, which not all writers are – including me). If you don't want to go public, how about inviting some friends round to your house, and in exchange for some food and drink, asking them to listen to you read from your work in progress? You can get good feedback from this, and it can also give you a huge confidence boost if you get a positive reaction.

Better yet, why not take one of your scenes and write it up as if it were part of a play? If there are several characters involved, you can ask your friends to play certain parts, involving them in the exercise and all having a jolly good time in the process (hopefully). Of course, if you haven't spent much time on the scene and it's a bit rubbish, it can still be fun – mainly because it will make everyone laugh, though maybe not for the right reasons. Seeing your scene come to life (however it goes down) will give you a rush, and it'll no doubt motivate you to sit down and write more (and maybe have some more evening readings). It'll also help you to iron out a few problems, especially bits that don't make sense to other people and any dialogue that may sound wooden or unnatural (unless that's just the way your friends speak, in which case, use your judgement). This is what people did before they had the Internet, you know, so it can help you get away from that screen for an evening too.

Fun Activities

The idea of writing a full-length novel can be daunting, but it doesn't have to be this way. It can – in fact – be fun! And it *should* be fun, if you want to be a writer. Of course, some parts of the process are more enjoyable than others, and here are a few activities and exercises you can do to get yourself in the zone, and hopefully have some fun in the process.

Write To Your Favourite Author

Here's a fun little task to do – write to your favourite author. OK, so this may not work if your favourite author is so famous that they would never have time to reply to each bit of their fan mail, but if you don't try you don't know, and sometimes just the act of writing the letter can be enough to get you motivated. Think of one of your favourite authors and pen them a letter (or email if you want to be all modern about it). Tell them why you admire them, which book of theirs is your favourite and how they inspired you to start writing yourself. If a particular sentence of theirs made an impact on your life, tell them. If their book lifted you up during a particularly crappy day, tell them. If you learnt something from them, either writing-wise or life-wise, tell them. Even if you never send it (and I think you should anyway) this exercise can really get you thinking about the power of writing, and it can motivate you to write your book so that one day, who knows? Maybe you'll get a fan letter or email of your own! This can be part of the whole 'visualising your future' exercise.

The Writing's On The Wall

I've mentioned sticking things up on your wall (or wherever) next to where you write to motivate you (and there's a bit of a silly section in the appendix on this very subject). I find this can be very inspiring and motivational, and as well as using things to get you thinking about your future writing and books, you can also use things from the past to give you that little bit of a boost. For example, when I first started releasing my books, my local newspaper ran a feature on me called 'The Profile' where they interview a local 'person of interest'. I have it framed on my wall above my desk as it was the first mention of me as a writer in a publication (and they asked me rather than the other way around, which is always a great feeling!). This piece obviously has the date on it (and it states my age at the time of writing), and whenever I'm freaking out or thinking I shouldn't be spending time on my own writing and should instead be focusing solely on my business, or every time I think about giving up on a book, I can look at that piece and be reminded not only of the time I was interviewed, but also of how far I've come, and how many books I've released since that date – how much I've accomplished since I was 26.

If you have anything like this, I suggest putting it in a

nice frame and sticking it on your wall, or on your desk, or just propped up next to your computer – whatever works. Even if it's just a flyer you've made yourself, or an author business card you've had done to give to potential readers, put it up there and give it a little glance every so often. It should give you a little boost every time.

As well as potential book covers and inspirational quotes of all kinds, there are lots of other things you can put up to motivate and inspire you when you hit a creative block:

- A picture of the cover of your favourite book.
- A picture of your favourite author or favourite character.
- Infographics about writing – statistics and so on regarding self-publishing or information regarding book sales of your favourite authors.
- If you've already got books out there and have been receiving reviews, why not put a few of them onto a page and stick it on your wall? Bonus points if the reviews are from people you don't know rather than friends and family (although any reviews are nice if they're good ones).
- 3D mock-ups of your book cover to really picture what it'll look like.
- Inspirational quotes from famous people, and also ones you've just heard and liked.
- Any encouraging emails from friends/family/fans about your writing.
- A picture representing why you're doing this. It may be down to fame and/or fortune – there's

nothing wrong with that – or it may be because you're dedicating the book to someone (in which case, put a photo of them on the wall to help you get motivated), or you may be proving to someone you can do it (again, the same thing, unless it's someone you really don't want staring down at you while you work).

Find more ideas in the appendix section, 'Your Writing Wall'.

Take A Few Steps In Your Characters' Shoes

If you're stuck with your writing – say, if you don't know how one of your characters would react in a certain situation, or you're not sure what should happen at a certain point in your story – then why not pretend to be one of your characters? This is a bit like the visualisation technique I mentioned, but with looking at your characters instead of yourself. How about doing things that your characters do in your story (especially if it's not something you usually do on a regular basis)?

If they hang out a lot at a local pub, go and do the same (although watch how many drinks you have – this is meant for research!). Sit at the bar and see what kind of people you come across: who's there with a partner and who's there with a group of friends? Who's there on an awkward first date and who's there with a bunch of people from work they don't necessarily like? Just see what happens – you might find inspiration for your story, and you might get into the mind of your character more.

Obviously, it goes without saying (though I'll say it

anyway) that if your character is a mass murderer, don't try and go down that route... and don't start breaking into places or stealing from people just to see what your character thinks like...! Stick to normal, easy things to achieve. Is your main character always going for long walks to think over the problems in their life? Go for a long walk. Is one of your main characters obsessed with going to the gym? Do a lot of scenes take place there? It might be worth heading over to your local leisure centre (if you're not already a regular). Just putting yourself in similar situations can get your mind going, and you may find it easier to set your scenes in certain places after you've spent a lot of time in similar locations. Plus, you might meet some new people – which is always nice – and you can legitimately label the time spent doing this as 'procrastiworking'.

Your Book Dedication

Dedicating your book to someone can be difficult, especially if it's your first book and you're not sure who to dedicate it to – or what to say – but having this in mind while writing your book can really help to focus you, and to motivate you to get it finished. Just picture the look on their face when they see a book dedicated to them – it'll all be worth it! Not many people get books dedicated to them, after all, so it really is a very special thing. Do the same with the acknowledgments page: keep a note of who you're going to thank at the end of the book, and keep thinking back to this when writing – think how pleased they'll be that they got a mention in your novel! Depending on whom you're thanking, this can be a great way to get motivated.

While it can be a nice surprise to present someone with

a book that's dedicated to them, one way to ensure you're going to finish it is by telling the person beforehand. They'll probably be so grateful and excited that it'll spur you on in your writing, and every time you think about quitting, you won't – not unless you want to seriously disappoint your friend or family member! They may even keep asking you how the book is going, giving you more motivation to sit down and write. You don't want to embarrass yourself (and them) by telling them all about your book and dedication, only to find that you never finish it, and never have a book to present to them. Just thinking about this awful result could be all you need to complete your novel. It sounds a little silly, yes, but if you're a nice person, you'll do everything in your power to make sure your friend's hopes aren't dashed.

It's also worth mentioning that dedicating your book to someone who has passed can also be a good motivator, as well as it being a lovely thing to do. Dedicating it to someone who's no longer with us means you are writing the book in their memory, and that will make you want to finish it, and to make it good.

Whatever you do and whomever you dedicate your book to, I believe this should be something you think about before you start writing, instead of just picking someone at random at the end. It works really well if the book features subjects that your dedicated person would be interested in, but you don't have to match them both at all if you don't want to. Just choose someone meaningful to dedicate your book to, and then have this person in mind as you're writing.

Get Gimmicky With Non-Fiction

Writing non-fiction can sometimes help you out with your fiction writing, especially if you're writing about something you either know about, or have actually done. Take this series of books, for example. After a year of working on my fiction projects when I could, I decided to write these books, and when I sat down I found that the words just flowed onto the page. This is not something I'd experienced with my own writing for any extended period of time, but because I was writing about things I'd done myself, and because I already knew most of it (I've had to do some research and I've had to use the Internet to find certain links, but that's about it), I found I could just sit and write, and get between 5,000 – 10,000 words written every day.

This is definitely not something that ever happens with my fiction (I believe my personal best for one day of writing one of my novels was 8,000 words, and that took me all day, compared to a few hours with these books). So, even if you have no intention of publishing a non-fiction book, it can be a great way of getting into the habit of sitting down and writing.

Why not start writing your memoirs as a bit of a fun exercise? After all, what do you know better than your own life? Start with recent events if your memory isn't too good, or go on Facebook and look back over your photo albums, taking each album and writing a paragraph, or a page, or several pages, based on those images. It can be a fun thing to do anyway (I love looking back over my old photos), and getting words down on the page is a great feeling, no matter what you're writing about. Plus, if you keep doing it, within a few months you could actually have a pretty decent life story written up, something you can publish in the future if you wish.

You're probably wondering what the 'gimmicky' part of this subheading is, aren't you? Well, when thinking about non-fiction and writing exercises – and 'writing what you know' or what you do – my mind immediately jumped to Danny Wallace, and his books *Yes Man*, *Awkward Situations For Men* and *What Not to Do (And How to Do It)*. I'm thinking particularly of *Yes Man* here, and even if you haven't read the book, you may well have seen the film version (which is pretty different but with a similar message) starring Jim Carrey and Zooey Deschanel. The basic premise is that Danny Wallace started saying yes to everything, taking him to some weird and wonderful places, and doing some weird and wonderful things. In the opening pages of his book he says that it started by him keeping a diary (something I'll go into more next), and that from writing down his experiences, this then turned into the final book. He thought of doing something a little 'out there' (saying yes to everything), did it, and recorded what he did in a creative, funny, and thought-provoking way.

Now, I'm not saying you have to go around saying yes to everything just so you can write about it (which you shouldn't anyway, as it's already been done), but I'm using it as an example of something you can do yourself. Think of something a little out there, do it, then write about it (preferably while it's still fresh in your mind). Keep a log of all the things you do as you do them (either with a diary, a blog, or simply just with photographs) so you've got something to refer back to, then sit down and write. Even if you never do anything with it, you'll have some great stories to tell at parties, and you could even turn it into a blog series or something else, if you didn't want to do a full-scale book.

The point is: do something great, then write about it. It could be anything, and the crazier the better (although don't go too extreme – I don't want you breaking any bones and then blaming it on me). Try and do one crazy thing a day for a year, or just one new thing a day for a year. Visit new places, randomly get on buses and see where you end up, talk to people in the middle of town instead of ignoring them... even small things can make a huge impact, and the more you do, the more you'll have to write about. Of course, you don't have to stick to non-fiction – the strange and new things you end up doing might give you ideas for a new novel, or for scenes in the novel you're stuck on. Do stuff. Write. Repeat.

Keep A Diary

I've just mentioned this with Danny Wallace, but even if you don't think you're doing a whole lot with your life, keeping a daily diary can be an invaluable resource for a writer, even if it takes years to come to anything. You'll definitely be glad you decided to keep a diary if you ever decide to write your autobiography, and even the most mundane-seeming day can give an insight into someone's life, and can remind you of things that you otherwise would have forgotten. Why not go even further and keep a scrapbook? Include notes and diary entries, but also make use of photographs, ticket stubs, and brochures of places you've visited.

So many people create scrapbooks for their holidays,

but not for their daily lives – as if their normal life isn't worth documenting, but it *so* is. Think of all the people who lived and died before things like video and other technologies were available. We'll never know much of their everyday lives, especially those people who were poor and couldn't therefore read or write – with no one to tell their stories, their memories died with them. We have the brilliant opportunity these days to not only record our lives, but to create something with them that we can leave behind when we're gone. This is why I get a lot of people asking me to help them write their life stories, so they can pass them on to their children and grandchildren and so on, and a lot of people leave it until the ends of their lives to start writing everything down before it's gone. Start early, keep a diary, and why not write your life story as you go along? When you get to a certain age, you'll find you've already written everything from your past, and you can share your life with your family before you're gone. This subject's a bit morbid, yes, but it's important, and at the very least, it's a writing exercise you can carry on throughout your life, whenever you feel like it.

Dreams

Now I don't know about you, but I've had some incredibly bizarre dreams over the years, and once I've got over the question of 'Just what is wrong with my subconscious?!' I've actually used some of these ideas in my books. After all, it was my mind that came up with them, so why not make some use out of them?

Not everyone dreams – or remembers them – to the same level, but I'm sure we've all had at least a few dreams (or nightmares) that we just couldn't shake, for whatever reason. So skim through your memory banks and note down any you can remember, or start keeping a dream diary. This doesn't have to be as 'Teenage girl' as it sounds – it could just mean noting down some keywords on the notes section of your phone when you wake up. Occasionally you might dream of something you can use to kick start your novel, whether directly or indirectly, if it sends your mind off on a random tangent you would never otherwise have thought of.

I've used several of my dreams as a basis for stories or scenes in my novels. For example, my short story *The Etiquette Of Being A Ghost* (published in my first short story collection, *Grown By The Wicked Moon*) was based on a particularly weird dream I had when I went back to university and the only course available was 'the etiquette of being a ghost'. Nothing really happened in the dream – in fact, I think I woke up before I attended a single class – but the name stuck with me when I woke up, and it got me thinking. Obviously, the first thing I thought was: what's wrong with me? But then my writer brain kicked in and I started thinking about the course – why would you need a course like that? Why would ghosts need classes about anything? Didn't we have to deal with these kinds of things – schools, uni, office meetings – enough when we were alive? And from that came my rather silly story.

I actually use the idea of dreams a lot in my books and stories, particularly in my Little Forest paranormal mystery series, where my main character – Beth Powers – develops some rather useful skills in terms of her dreams. They can also be a great plot device to show what your characters are thinking and what's worrying them, even if they don't realise it themselves within the story. Dreams are great to experiment with in writing.

Even if you don't think it will help, why not try keeping a dream diary for a few weeks and see what happens? It might actually start training your brain to remember more of your dreams (which may or may not be a good thing depending on the kinds of things you dream about), and it may well give you some inspiration for your writing. It can be fun to do, anyway, so why not give it a shot?

Hang Out With Friends

If all else fails, forget about the computer and your crafts and your lists and your music for a while and gather up some of your nearest and dearest. This can work as simply a social distraction from your writing (especially if you've been locking yourself away for days on end trying to get something down on paper), but it can also help you with developing your ideas – if your friends are up for it, anyway.

Tell them of your idea for the book, and get a discussion going on the characters, the locations, and the storylines. Record the conversation so you'll be able to refer back to the ideas, and when you come to start writing, your head should already be filled with information regarding your book. Of course, remember to credit your friends if you decide to use any of their ideas or perspectives! Two heads really can be better than one, and three better than two, and so on, and you can use your friends or families to help you in various different ways when it comes to your book (again, assuming they're willing). Show them a drawing of one of your characters, or a photograph you found on the

Internet, and see what ideas they come up with for their personality. Show them a picture of the location you're using and see what they think – they may have ideas you hadn't even thought of.

Then there are the silly games you can get into. Go around your friends and each say a word in a sentence, with the idea being to create some kind of story. For example, the first person says 'one', the next says 'day', and the person after that says 'Sharon' or another name, before going on to say what Sharon got up to that day. Most of the time it'll be nonsense, but sometimes it can give you ideas, especially if you're trying to do it around the characters and settings in your book.

You can also try Consequences – that classic game where you write a man's name, a woman's name, where they met, what he said, what she said, and the consequences. Each time you write something, you fold the piece of paper down and pass it onto the next person, and so on, until you end up with a story. My family used to play this at Christmas, and inevitably – depending on how much alcohol had been consumed – you'd end up with a highly inappropriate story to be telling to all your family members, but it was always fun to do. Try it out with a limited number of male and female names – e.g. the names of your characters – and try and set it in the world of your story. You'll probably get a lot of rude and crude tales, but getting used to thinking of your characters as people who can do and say anything can really help when it comes to writing your novel. Plus, you may actually get some good ideas.

Murder Mysteries

Maybe it's just me and the kind of genres I like reading and writing in, but I love murder mysteries no matter what form they come in, and I've participated in several fictional ones myself over the years. From a do-it-at-home one at a friend's house where we each got a crappy prop to go with our characters, to an alien-themed one at a hotel which included a lovely meal, to an Irish-themed one (with hilariously awful accents) at a place in Denver, where the alcohol was most definitely flowing. They're great when you're thinking about storylines and writing as they all follow a very similar plot structure, and it can be interesting to see how different characters are used within the story. It's a fun thing to go to with a load of friends anyway, but what I'm suggesting here is even more fun (or I think so, at least).

Have you ever been to one of these events and thought, 'I could come up with a better mystery than this' or 'I could write a better script than this one'? If so, why not create your own murder mystery party? You can take the book you're working on and transform it into a short, fun script. It doesn't have to be anything fancy – just invite a few of your friends round and provide nibbles and food – but it can be a great way of testing out your own characters and plots, especially if your novel is a murder mystery or has 'whodunit' or crime elements in it. Even if you don't actually end up putting on the murder mystery party, it can be great fun writing the script, and you might see flaws in your characters and storylines that you didn't notice before. The magic, however, most definitely happens when you *do* put it on as a murder mystery party.

To make it more authentic, give your friends some

props or parts of costumes to help them get into character. You don't have to spend a lot of time and money on this – you can grab things from charity shops or see what's lying around the house – and even just the act of thinking about what your characters would wear and the types of things they'd own can get the creative juices flowing.

When it comes to the actual murder mystery night, the way your friends portray their characters can get you thinking about them in a different light (and maybe thinking about your friends in a different light as well!) and if there's something wrong with your story, or there's a massive plot hole, it will soon become apparent. Better now with your friends than in a few months' time when it's up on Amazon waiting to be purchased and downloaded. It will also give you an idea as to how obvious your ending is and how many people guessed it (although obviously you will have to simplify your book a lot to get your plot into a murder mystery party script). Whatever ends up happening, it's all good writing practice, with a bit of fun thrown in too.

Get Writing, No Matter What

Of course, the main thing we want to get you doing is actually writing, and as I've mentioned, sometimes it's the very act of sitting down and typing that seems to bring on our creative/mental blocks. So, we just need to get used to writing, no matter what and no matter how we do it. Here are some more ideas.

Don't Start At The Start

The beginning. Ah, yes, that first killer line you need to hook the reader in, the first few pages where boring words and boring scenes will result in your reader flinging the book at the wall in disgust (or at least just choosing a different book on their e-reader). There are endless lists out there detailing the best and worst first lines of novels over the years, and I don't know about you, but reading about them can sometimes make me feel even more nervous about how my own novels start. The way you finish your book is vitally important too, of course, but if the reader never gets past the first page, you don't really have to worry about their opinion on the ending, as they'll never actually get to it. Depressing, isn't it? Writing the first pages of your novel can be really, really hard.

But – and there's always a but – you don't have to start a novel by writing the start. After all, the beginning and end of your book will probably be the hardest bits to write – you have to hook the reader in with the former and bring the narrative to a satisfying conclusion with the latter – so why torture yourself with them if you're not getting anywhere? If you're having difficulties getting into the story, why not start somewhere in the middle instead? Do you have an idea for an epic scene that comes later on, one that is exciting and interesting and therefore possibly easier to write? Even if you don't know all the details yet, you can still get words down on the page and add to it later.

Just write the part of your book you're most excited about – you'll start getting your word count up and it might just get you into the zone so much that you then go on to write the beginning straight away afterwards. Well, you never know. In a similar vein, try writing parts you're more comfortable with first. If you find dialogue easy to write, start with a talk-heavy scene, whereas if you find action easier to write, start with the scene where the hero leaps from that burning building or narrowly misses getting caught up in an explosion. When it comes to first drafts, you don't have to do things chronologically. In fact, logic might not come into the first draft at all (it rarely does with mine)!

Write What You Know

This is a massive cliché, but it's a cliché for a reason. Obviously, there are people out there who believe that you absolutely should write what you *don't* know –

after all, how many people can say they've been in space? Or talked to the dead? Or had an out-of-body experience? Yet we get sci-fi, fantasy, and horror books a plenty. I'm not saying stick to what you know completely and exclusively, just use experiences from your past to build up or enhance a story. I do this a lot – both in my short stories and my novels – and it's fun to take a situation that really happened and build its own story around it.

One of my short stories in *Grown By The Wicked Moon – Apocalypse 101 –* was based on a zombie riot training activity day I attended at an industrial park in the midlands. Obviously, there were no actual zombies present, but I have to say I was surprised at the 'zombies' they presented to us. These weren't the slow, bumbling *Night Of The Living Dead* type zombies, these were fast, furious, and huge – they tackled you to the ground, lay on top of you, and wouldn't let you go. The whole day was absolutely exhausting but it did make me think. How would I act in a zombie apocalypse (or any type of apocalypse, for that matter)? Would I be able to defend myself? Of course, the only weapons we got given on the activity day were a shield and a baton – the middle part of which fell out of mine, leaving me with nothing more than a floppy piece of foam to defend myself with. What would happen if you could actually defend yourself at these training days? What if you *had to* defend yourself? The idea of a real zombie apocalypse training camp came to mind and the story was written.

I've used a lot of my experiences when writing my novels as well. In the fifth instalment of the Little Forest paranormal mystery series, *The Gloaming*, I drew on my trip to some caves when I was in Colorado, as well as mixing in some other experiences I had while travelling in Asia, from visiting a cave in Ha Long Bay to squeezing myself through the Cu Chi tunnels further down in Vietnam. This mixture of experiences came together to form the gang's visit to the spooky Ballycave cave in Ireland. As the series is heavily based on the paranormal, I added in a few extra things, but I did take a lot from my experiences: the feeling of claustrophobia when going through the tunnels, the huge cavernous places that seemed to go on for miles, and the eerie feeling that you weren't alone.

In *The Gloaming*, there is also a fire that happens at a large event, and I took a lot of what happened during this scene from a video I saw during my fire marshal training day when I worked at the NHS. It was a horrific video showing an actual fire in an actual venue in America, and a person with a video camera actually picked up the people trying to get out of the building, jumping on each other and effectively killing each other as much as the smoke was killing them. Even though the video stopped abruptly after that, it stayed in my mind for days – well, years in fact, as it was several years later that I used it as inspiration when writing my scene. Of course, yet again I embellished on this, adding in little details such as paranormal elements to fit it in with the rest of the book.

Another thing I drew on in my Little Forest series was an experience I had as a teenager. This takes place in the second book of the series, *Memento Mori*: in this scene, the main character Beth Powers is horrified when she wakes up to find herself paralysed and unable to breathe. She feels like someone invisible is lying on top of her, pinning her to the bed. This happened to me when I was 18, and it is not something you easily forget. It didn't help that I remembered seeing a *Strange But True?* type TV programme on a similar incident, where a woman saw an old hag in the corner of the room and was convinced it was this woman who was lying on top of her, trying to squeeze the life out of her. I had this in mind at the time, and needless to say, I was sufficiently freaked out. After researching the phenomenon, I found that it was called 'sleep paralysis' and that it was also sometimes referred to as 'the hag phenomenon'. In the context of the book, I could give it much more of a supernatural feel, something which added to the creepiness of the whole scene.

Another main thing I used as inspiration for one of my books was in the first of the series, *The Former World*. This story involves the main character going on a ghost tour in Edinburgh, where she and the rest of the tour group get locked inside a very small and very dark mausoleum in a graveyard. This happened to me when I went on a ghost tour in Edinburgh, although it was a small cell in the graveyard grounds rather than a mausoleum. When I was there, the tour guide talked of how some people on these tours come away with strange marks and scratches on their skin that they can't explain, and this gave me the idea for something that ended up being the basis of the entire first book in the series.

I also used my previous occupations as inspiration for the characters in my books. For example, my main character works in her little local cinema, something which I did for just over a year. She also does some temping in data entry, which I've also done in the past more than once. As I said, it doesn't have to be anything huge; you can simply use your own experiences as a basis for what happens to the characters. It will give those scenes some authenticity.

Another of my short stories, *Darkford Hall*, was based on a ghost hunting experience I went on in a well known stately home/theme park in the midlands, and while I didn't quite come across any ghostly activity like they did in the story, it did give me an idea of how those types of evenings were run, and what equipment they used.

Locations are extremely important when it comes to novels – or any other story you may be writing – and I've used many local and not-so-local places as ideas (please note: I haven't 'copied' the places, just used them for inspiration). In my Little Forest series, I based a lot of locations in the fictional county on real-life attractions and buildings, while tweaking them and changing them for my own use within the stories. For example, in Little Forest there is a castle that looks down over the village, something that brings in the tourists, and by being surrounded by the Great Specton woods, it is a locality that is used a lot during the spooky outdoor scenes. While it doesn't really resemble the local castle in my hometown, it certainly has elements that are the same. I also set a scene at a large stately house that puts on a Hallowe'en event, something that was inspired by the stately home in my home village. Again, there are major differences, but my own childhood spent attending similar events at the real stately home was definitely in my mind as I wrote about the grand mansion house and the beautiful gardens.

To some extent, I also based the village of Little Forest on my own home village, although not in any obvious ways. My home village isn't quite as cool as Little Forest for one thing – there's no diner or cinema or gig venue – but it does have that same small town/village feel to it, that rural community atmosphere where everyone knows everyone else and where secrets aren't kept secrets for long. Think about where you grew up (or where you live now) – are there any elements you can use when coming up with locations for your stories? It doesn't matter if they're big things or small things, they can really help to round out a place when you're doing your world building.

History, of course, is another resource we can use, especially local history. I live in a small town in the midlands, and the towns and villages around it – like most places in England – have their own myths and folk tales. Some of the strange stories are even true – usually the less believable ones! – and I've drawn on several in my Little Forest series, which heavily relies on the folklore that surrounds the English countryside. One of the main stories explored in the series is the life of a doctor in the 1800s who (allegedly) poisoned his patients, friends, and family members. This is based on the life of William Palmer, a doctor who lived in the nearby town of Rugeley and worked (and was hanged) in Stafford. It's a deliciously dark tale, and one that is well known in the area. Much like in Staffordshire in real life, I've given the story of the evil doctor a big part to play in the fictional county of Covershire in my books. Head down to your local library and start investigating the area you live in – you might be surprised at what you find.

Here's a little exercise to help get you in the creative mood: make a list of all of the weird and wonderful experiences you've ever had, even if you have no intention at the moment of using them in your writing, as they could come in handy in the future. These can be both good and bad, wonderful memories from holidays and awful things that happened that have stayed with you, no matter what the reason. Obviously, what you can make the most use out of will heavily depend on what genre you're writing in (spooky occurrences may not help in a straightforward romance book, for instance), but you never know – with a bit of tweaking, these real life experiences could find their way into your work, adding an authenticity to the scene that it may otherwise not have had. Do the same with locations that have had an effect on you – no matter what that effect was – as they could come in useful.

Fanfiction

Fanfiction – or fanfic – is huge on the Internet, and if you don't know what it is, I'm assuming you've actually been living under a rock for the past ten years or so. There are whole online communities devoted to fanfic for films, TV shows and more; a fanfic writer basically takes a ready-made 'world' with existing characters (say, from a film or a game) and writes their own story within that world. They can add their own characters and set existing characters in different times and locations, but essentially they are 'borrowing' the characters and places that have already been created by someone else. If you're really into a TV show or film, it can be a great way of writing the stories you'd want to see happen to your favourite characters, and you're pretty much guaranteed a captive audience (if you're a good writer, anyway) as there are avid readers of fanfic just as there are avid writers of fanfic. Another advantage of fanfiction stories is that you can do 'crossovers', mixing two shows or two worlds into one story and seeing what you'd really love to see happen to characters who in TV or film would never actually meet.

If you want to get into writing but the idea of a full-on original novel just seems like far too much to do, then beginning with fanfic could be the way in for you. Just start small and simple: pick your favourite film or TV show, something where you know the characters inside out – what they'd say, what they'd wear, what they'd think, how they'd act – and come up with your own story surrounding them. If you don't think you're that great at dialogue, write a dialogue-heavy scene, and the same with action or romance, or whatever else you think you need to improve on. Once you're finished with your story, find an online forum/community and upload it (checking the terms and conditions first). Hopefully you'll get some feedback – both about the fanfic and about your writing in general – and you can then use this to improve your writing the next time. It's a bit like attending a writer's group, but be careful – only ask for feedback if you're sure you know the characters and the world in which your story is set. Fanfic readers can be a bit fanatical (no surprises there going by the name), and you want to focus on getting writing feedback rather than getting into an argument about how out of character your protagonist is being.

One of the first things I wrote (and finished) was actually a fanfic about *Buffy The Vampire Slayer* when I was pretty young. It wasn't great, but it got me into writing, and finishing that story gave me a real sense of achievement. It's often easier to get to the end of a short fanfic story than the end of your first novel, so why not give it a try? If you're not sure, have a read of some first. Pick your favourite show, and Google their fanfic universe. Here are just a few ideas of sites to look at:

FanFiction.Net
Quotev - www.quotev.com
Kindle Worlds - kindleworlds.amazon.com
Feedbooks - www.feedbooks.com
Wattpad - www.wattpad.com

These are also listed in the Resources section.

Now, I'm no expert on fanfiction, but I do have a writer friend – Lauren K Nixon – who loves fanfic and who understands how it can help you become a better writer. I asked her to write some words on the topic and here they are – enjoy!

Now, I know what you're thinking: "Oh God, not fanfiction!" But bear with me!

If you don't know what fanfiction is, first of all: really? Fanfiction is a collection of stories, poetry, songs and general writings based in the world of or involving the characters of a favourite book, film, television programme, musical, comic or game. It's been around for decades, but enjoyed something of a boost in popularity following the phenomenal success of a series of books and films set in a particular magical school (you know the one, boys and girls!) No one profits from fanfiction, because that would be a breach of copyright of the original author – though there are rare exceptions to this.

It's possible if you are new to the concept, that you will have heard negative things about it.

Don't get me wrong, as a long-term reader of fanfiction, I know what horrors lurk at the depths of each category, whether it's a pairing that is not only unlikely, but probably illegal in several countries, a poor understanding of human (or other) anatomy, or an insistence on having your favourite characters sing pop music, there is something there to offend, disgust or disturb anyone.

And don't even get me started on the writers who believe that the three 'p's are optional (punctuation, paragraphs and plot).

But for all that, fanfiction can be a source of extraordinary creativity and incredible writing – you just have to know where to look.

From a writer's point of view, fanfiction is a great way to develop writing skills. The familiar world and characters of your favourite book or film can create a 'safe' or 'comfortable' backdrop to play around with.

When I first realised that writing was what I wanted to do, I decided to challenge myself: if I could write a novel-length fanfiction in a reasonable amount of time, to a reasonable standard (being, in my mind, one which didn't make me cringe too much when I re-read it later), with a fairly complex plot, then I would know I could trust myself to do the same thing with an original story.

Following the core of an established plot made that first foray into serious (hah) writing a lot less scary – as did the knowledge that the people reading it would already be interested in the topic.

Of course, once I'd written one, another story idea presented itself and really, it was a bit too much fun to ignore! That's the thing about writing – particularly for fanfiction – if you're not enjoying it, there's no point doing it. The more I wrote, the more adventurous I began to get: I planned out longer story arcs, incorporating several themes into series of fics.

I set myself deadlines: I began to write larger sections of each story in one sitting, arranging things so I could publish one chapter per week. I can tell you, there is nothing so frightening than that self-imposed deadline looming, especially when you realise that there are people actually waiting for an update.

Yes.

In writing silly stories to develop my writing skills and get me into a rhythm of writing every day (or at least several times a week) I had managed to find an audience. It's really quite daunting realising that people actually care about what you write; daunting and incredibly rewarding.

I started getting reviews – and not just people telling me they liked my work, there were also people who gave constructive criticism. I messaged them back – I still do, every week – and found a group of people who are not afraid to speak their mind, but will fill your inbox with complaints if you accidentally miss a week. They teach you the power of writing – not just in terms of spreading ideas, but they also remind you how a story can pick you up by the heart and take you to places you never expected to go.

It is possible to get a bit giddy when you know you're toying with your readers' emotions – I must admit, somewhat guiltily, that I get a little buzz when someone tells me I've "Got them right in the feelz." And oh – the power of a cliff-hanger. There have been times, dear readers, when I have actually cackled maniacally when releasing a particular chapter – but don't worry, I'm much better now! The reader-writer relationship goes both ways, of course.

Every week I sit on tenterhooks after updating my current fanfic, waiting for these lovely reviewers. It's a cliché in fanfiction circles, but they really do make your world go around. I don't know if they realise it, but those reviewers have been some of my strongest supporters, offering encouragement, criticism and plot ideas. One or two of them have become long-term friends.

As with any online medium, you do inevitably get the odd troll, but it's always fairly obvious who they are, and they're easily ignored for the most part. The great thing about the fanfiction community is that it stands up for writers under fire from trolls; most fanfiction websites also allow you to report, remove or block reviewers who are clearly just there to be offensive.

Writing fanfiction has pushed me to develop my skills in several unexpected directions: last year, for example, I began writing short stories for the first time, inspired by one or two of my fellow fanfiction authors. I'm currently experimenting with a series of thrillers – a genre I never thought I'd get into – which I wouldn't have even dreamed of working on if I hadn't been involved in fanfiction.

It's also a great way to while away the time between finishing your first novel and hearing from any of the agents you've applied to. Think of it as a means of keeping your hand in while you're waiting for your next story idea to fully mature.

The majority of authors, movie makers and TV producers don't have strong feelings about fanfiction, but there are one or two who don't like people playing with their characters, so do check who they are before setting out on your first fanfiction experiment. There is usually a list of these in the publication section of whichever site you have chosen to write for – if you haven't spotted this, then you need to go back and read the terms and conditions again, because you clearly weren't paying attention!

Fanfiction can be a rewarding way to build up your writing skills, but the real value of it is the tremendous capacity for silliness, which should never be underestimated. Writing is a means of expressing yourself – and sometimes a means of exploring aspects of the world that you find it hard to talk about out loud. Fanfiction offers a safe environment for new (and particularly young) writers to try new things, get feedback, develop, and make long lasting friendships with people all over the world and from all walks of life.

Give it a go!

Thanks to Lauren K Nixon for her words on fanfiction. If you'd like to check out any of her work, you can find it on <u>fanfiction.net</u> under the pseudonym of 'Parlanchina'. And once you've read some fanfic, maybe you'll want to try it out for yourself. What have you got to lose?

Writing Blogs

If you're serious about writing, you've probably read a lot of blog posts on the subject, but have you considered writing your own blog? It doesn't have to be writing related, or even literature related – just as long as you post regularly and use it to enhance your writing skills. If you end up with a bit of a following, even better!

Blogs can be an alternative to writing a diary every day (although you might want to spend a bit more time editing it as other people will be able to read it, and while we're at it, maybe don't write down your deepest, darkest secrets if you're going to publish it online), and just the act of sitting down and writing regularly will help you when you come to write your novel.

Even if your blog isn't directly related to writing, you can use it to refer to your novels and other work if you're writing something that links with the subjects and themes in your books. I've put a couple of examples of my previous blog posts in the appendix so you can see how I linked my blog to my novels, and I'm going to put one here now so you have more of an idea of what I mean (this was written a couple of years ago):

Medium Rare: Magic and Mysticism in Fiction and

Life

My 'Little Forest' series of novels ('The Former World', 'Memento Mori' and 'The Exalted') focus on aspects of the paranormal which, for most people, are only found in the realm of fiction: communicating with the dead, clairvoyance, telepathy, extrasensory perception, and other magical and mystical powers that seemingly only belong in the pages of a horror or fantasy book.

I, like many other authors, take inspiration from popular culture, modern society and contemporary artists, but even though 'The Former World' and the other books in my series are set in modern-day England, I had to take a long, dark journey into the past to start my research. A metaphorical journey, of course; while I may be open to ideas of the supernatural, I don't claim to be able to travel back in time. Yet...

Hundreds of years ago, it was quite normal to be walking down the street in your village and to overhear gossip about the local cunning-man or cunning-woman: people who claimed to be able to find your lost or stolen property, identify criminals, or cure you of an ailment, all by magical means. At least, I'm guessing it was normal – as I said, I don't actually have a time machine (yet).

My point is, people in the sixteenth, seventeenth, eighteenth, and even nineteenth centuries believed in normal-looking people who had extraordinary powers. They believed in curses, spells, divination, magic, and necromancy. It was a mystical world, where the forests were home to hermits calling themselves wizards, where the country seemed much bigger and the medical options much smaller, where magic was something that was not only believed in, but was actually extremely common.

Fast forward to the twenty-first century. We still have wizards (although mainly in the form of fictional magical men), and we still have most of everything else – albeit in a much more diluted way – but there's one key thing that's missing (at least, for the majority of people): belief.

Now, I'm aware that some people believe in all of these paranormal subjects as much as our ancestors did hundreds of years ago, and I realise why, for others, that belief has faded – all of the advancements in science, the growing infrastructure and international media, instant access to information, logical explanations being provided for strange phenomena – but the mystery of it still intrigues me.

In my most recent novel in the Little Forest series, 'The Exalted', we meet a rather suspicious character, 'Marvin the Mystic' (real name, Terence). He claims to be able to speak to the dead, and embarks on a career of being a medium, ranging from private readings to dramatic theatre shows. This, of course, annoys the main character, Beth Powers, who knows for certain that he can't see the spirits he claims to be able to see. She doesn't like the fact that he's making money from (and taking the piss out of) vulnerable people – people who wish to hear from their dead loved ones – and that's the problem, really, isn't it?

We don't believe in magic and the supernatural because

we don't want to be taken for a ride, we don't want to be taken advantage of, we don't want to be made fun of or be made a fool of. In this day and age, this is understandable: you can barely do anything or go anywhere without people knowing about it. So-called friends tag you in places and photos on Facebook, they tweet what you're doing to an audience of thousands, they record you on their phone and upload it to Youtube to an audience of millions. A few hundred years ago, if you wanted to visit a cunning-man for help, you just wandered over to his hovel under cover of darkness, without having to worry about getting caught on CCTV or being pranked by some hidden-camera show.

I remember a television programme a few years ago made by the lovely Derren Brown: 'Derren Brown Investigates: The Man Who Contacts The Dead'. Now, I'll try not to gush too much, but I'm a massive fan of Derren. I've seen every single TV show he's ever done, and I've attended all but one of his amazing stage shows. If you haven't heard of him, you need to look him up: he's charming, he's funny, he's clever, and he has a deliciously dark streak... dastardly, you might say – just watch the recent 'Apocalypse' two-part special and you'll see what I mean. But his stunts, his tricks, his explorations and exposés always have a point to them, and of course, the point of 'The Man Who Contacts The Dead' was to highlight the fact that many mediums aren't what they claim to be. There has been, inevitably, a lot of controversy over this (as with most of Derren's shows – for example, he recently convinced a life-long atheist scientist of God's presence in just 15 minutes), and it just goes to show that even in the twenty-first century, there are people willing to stand up for both sides.

When I think about it, Derren has covered pretty much all of the themes and subjects which are explored in my Little Forest series (and in my own short stories – some of which have been released as a collection under the title 'Grown By The Wicked Moon'): talking to the dead, spiritualism, religion, zombie outbreaks (that's right, you heard me), psychology, manipulation, and the power one person can hold over another. Derren has made perfectly normal citizens stage an armed robbery, he's convinced someone that he committed a murder, and he manipulated a man into 'shooting' British national treasure, Stephen Fry. He's turned someone into a miraculous faith-healer, predicted the lottery numbers, staged a terrifying (and fake) séance, and played Russian Roulette live on television. He also made an entire town believe in a lucky dog statue, the devilish rogue (note: this wasn't the sole point of that particular show). It's quite a CV. I think his 'Investigates' show did a lot to change opinions on mediums, or at least it got people thinking about the subject who may not have come across it in their daily lives before. It warned the public of the possible crooks and frauds out there, and while I'm by no means against all mediums, the show was good for exposing how they went about their work.

My own personal views on spiritualism aside (which, if you're interested, is a lot of cynicism mixed with cautious optimism at the idea that bona fide mediums could exist, or at least have done in the past), I wanted to end with a suggestion.

The worlds of the paranormal, the supernatural, the afterlife, the mystical realms and the magical people, are all fascinating. It's a bit morbid, a bit sinister, and very intriguing. We love the idea of it, we love discussing it, we love questioning it and debating it until the wee hours when surrounded by friends and large quantities of alcohol. It is one of the ultimate questions: what happens to us when we die?

Mediums and fortune-tellers can be a bit of fun, and whether they're legit or not, they make for good entertainment. Like many people, I get uncomfortable when they start delivering specific messages from the dead – especially if those messages make the intended recipient burst into tears – but generally they fire up the imagination and get you wondering: could it be true?

As long as humans live, I think there will always be questions asked about the meaning of life, ponderings concerning what happens when we die, and wonderments regarding the possibility of talking to the dead. And personally, I hope that people never stop asking these questions, no matter what science may tell us in the future, and no matter how sceptical we become as a society. Because as long as we keep the prospect alive, we're somehow linking back to our ancestors, the ones who swept through the forest in long, black cloaks, hunting out the local wise men and muttering enchantments under their breath to keep away the evil. (I don't know about you, but if I lived in those times, I'd definitely make sure I wore a long, black coat. Preferably one that swooshed round corners dramatically – I'll get one ready for when someone invents time travel).

It is much like when I'm watching a magic show (the theatrical, rabbit-out-of-a-hat, lady-cut-in-half-while-

wearing-not-many-clothes type of magic show): although part of me wants to know how the tricks are done, part of me really doesn't. I like the mystery, I like the intrigue, I like the not knowing.

Most mediums and fortune tellers may well be fake, and as long as they're not hurting anyone, I'm OK with that. They're one of the last links to our mystical past, one of the last connections to the weird and wonderful world of spiritualism, one of the last reminders of just how strange the universe – and us humans – can be. I suggest that while we should keep our eyes open for people who may rip us off, we should also embrace the strangeness, embrace the past, and embrace the magic.

I don't know about you, but give me a bit of mystery any day.

Some writers even make money from their blogs, by recommending products or through affiliate schemes, not to mention gathering interested readers who then go on to buy their books. Of course, money shouldn't necessarily be your main aim when writing a blog, but if it happens then it's a great bonus.

Whatever you blog about, it can be a great exercise in writing regularly, so why not give it a shot?

Here are a few sites to check out if you're thinking of setting up a blog (these are also listed in the Resources section in the appendix):

Blogger - www.blogger.com
WordPress - www.wordpress.com
SquareSpace - www.squarespace.com

Tumblr - www.tumblr.com
Google+ - plus.google.com
Hubpages - www.hubpages.com
Medium - www.medium.com
Live Journal - www.livejournal.com
Joomla - www.joomla.org
Typepad - www.typepad.com

Type Nonsense

If you don't want to spend time writing in notepads or going on an inspirational walk, get straight into typing by sitting down, opening your word processor, and typing. Type anything – anything at all that comes to mind. For example, the first sentence to pop into your head: 'The man walked into the fish and chip shop and looked around suspiciously.' Just the very act of typing and seeing words appear on the screen can help get you into the zone, and who knows? Perhaps it'll even give you an idea – I'm now thinking of the dodgy things that could be happening in that fish and chip shop; is the man a detective? Is he after someone who works there? Is the place haunted? Is someone poisoning the chips? Just what the hell is going on?! It'll get your mind working, and that's what we want. Now I quite want to write about the fish and chips killer!

Of course, there's nonsense and then there's *nonsense*. Try sitting and typing absolutely anything, even if it doesn't make any sense. Remember the thing about monkeys with typewriters and how – given an infinite amount of time – they'd be able to type the entire works of Shakespeare? Now, I'm not comparing you to a monkey, but sometimes sitting and just hitting keys aimlessly can get you back into the motions of typing.

And hopefully, after a while, your nonsense will start to make sense (which is always good when you're a writer).

Typing nonsense really does get you used to the act of typing, which I think is what holds a lot of writers (especially but not exclusively first time writers) back; the mental block is waiting in the back of your mind, and as soon as you see a keyboard – or your hand touches a key – it's there, right at the front of your mind, taunting you. You try to type an opening sentence but just the very motion of trailing your fingers over those keys seems like too much, and all of a sudden you're wondering how on earth you thought you'd be able to write an entire novel when you can't even write two lines. So, start typing nonsense, and soon your brain will realise that you can, in fact, move your hands over those keys without hyperventilating or throwing up or whatever response you thought your body would have to this act, and that in time, the nonsense can become actual words, actual sentences, and an actual story.

Befriend A Ghost

Ghostwriting is a controversial subject. I ghostwrite myself (as part of my writing services), and I make sure I carefully choose the projects I work on. If someone has a life story they want to tell but don't know where to start, I'll gladly help them write their book. After all, it is the story that is important to them; they just want to find someone who can make it into a reality. A lot of these people who come to me have children and grandchildren who don't know their entire life story (do you know your grandparents' whole life stories? Very few do), and they want to get their stories down on paper before they die. This way, they can live on after they've passed, and their stories won't be lost or forgotten. It's very satisfying helping people with these kinds of books, and I wholeheartedly agree with ghosting these sorts of projects.

I also work with writers who, for various reasons, can't complete the book they are working on. They may have started it and then run into health issues, they may have most of the story but don't know how to finish it, or they may just need a little help getting back on the writing horse after a long time away from it. I love helping writers in this way, and seeing how others work also motivates me as well. What I don't agree with is people who want to be writers and make a living from writing, without actually writing a single word. If you can't write, spell, or construct sentences, why would you want to be a writer? I think this is cheating, and I won't work on these kinds of projects (after all, a novel takes a lot of time and effort to write, and if I put that much energy and soul into something, and if all of the ideas are mine, I don't want it to be credited to someone else).

With that in mind, if you're a writer, you probably won't want to hire a ghostwriter for anything, but even a paragraph or two written by someone else on your subject can get you out of that funk and help you to continue writing. It doesn't have to be a professional, either – give a friend or family member some notes and ask them to write a few sentences. This also might give you a different perspective on your characters that you hadn't thought of before. It can also be a good way of kick starting a project – if all you have are bullet points or mind maps of your ideas and storylines, having someone else write the first few pages can sometimes be all you need to get into the flow. Just make sure you either go back and rewrite those pages before attempting to publish, or get permission from your friend/whoever it was and credit them in the acknowledgements. Sometimes, it's just the tiniest push we need to get into the swing of things and get those words flowing onto the page, and when that happens, it's an incredible feeling.

Get Your Extras Written

When you're a writer and you're planning to release a book, there's a hell of a lot to think about, and a hell of a lot to write other than your actual novel. While some people leave all these extra little bits until they've finished their book and it's ready to go, there are some benefits to getting these things written up first, or at least while you're writing your book (don't worry, if things change you can always add to them/amend them later). The things I'm talking about here are your book blurb, your author biography, your book description, your sales pitch, your marketing copy, your press release... all these things need to be taken into account at some point, and you can do at least some of them before your book's finished (especially the author biography and vague book blurb/description).

The benefits of getting these done earlier rather than later include: preparation, motivation, and being able to build a 'buzz' around your upcoming book. If you're anything like me, you'll feel much better about things if you're prepared, and just the very act of writing sales copy for your novel should motivate you to get it finished – what's the point of spending all this time writing blurbs and press releases if you never even complete the thing?! Also, if you know you're definitely going to be releasing your book in the upcoming months or weeks, it helps to start building a 'buzz' around it as soon as possible. Get the cover out there, get the blurb out there, send out press releases to local publications and make people aware that you're releasing a book. Then, well, you kind of have to release it, don't you? There's nothing like a public deadline to get you working!

Even if you just write your blurb or your biography, you're telling your brain that this is something you're serious about, and hopefully you'll start to get in that writing zone quicker every time you sit down at your computer.

Writing Prompts

Writing prompts are a good way of getting you to start writing, even if it's nothing to do with the book you're planning and even if your little writing exercises never see the light of day. Start with the beginning of a story and continue from there, seeing where it leads you, or read about a theme or an idea for a story and get writing a short story or piece of flash fiction about it. There are several websites out there with writing prompts on, you can get daily emails with them on if you subscribe to a list, and there are a load of books you can buy to get you going (as well as apps and interactive websites that will prompt you to start writing). As an example and to give you an idea of how you can use writing prompts, I've listed some here, and they are also in the appendix so you can access them easily afterwards:

The Beginnings Of A Story

Take these first sentences and turn them into a short story, whether it's a fun tale or a sinister scenario:

- The night was cold, and the pitter-patter of

raindrops on the window was the only sound to be heard.

- This was it. This was Jimmy's big moment – this was his chance to show the world what he could do.
- 'Why did it always have to rain on Judgement Day?' thought Mark bitterly, as he looked up at the stormy sky.
- "Don't shoot!" shouted the policeman, holding his hands in the air.
- The walls of this room would always be grey; no matter what happened in the future, the past would always be here, soaked into the old bricks.
- When he woke from his dream, he was surprised to find that reality was far stranger than any of his nightmares could ever be.
- The balloon floated upwards into the cool night air, and she watched as it disappeared into the heavens.
- His teacher had always told him he'd never make anything of himself, that he'd never achieve anything in life. Well, he was going to show him.
- The cat jumped on her lap, purred, and settled down to sleep. She sighed as she stroked his soft fur; running the country would just have to wait.
- The keys on the keyboard were being pressed at lightning speed, the words of the novel pouring

onto the page. The only problem was – they were doing it on their own.

- The dog was barking at something in the trees, and as the man walked over to the drooping branches, he saw what was driving his collie crazy...

- When you haven't had a mirror for over ten years, seeing your reflection can come as something of a shock.

- All at once, the birds stopped tweeting, the dog stopped barking, and the comforting chatter of the television switched off. It was coming.

- When he opened his door that morning, the snow was so high he couldn't even see the sky. Shivering, he made his way into the cold – he couldn't be late for this meeting, no matter what happened.

- The empty box seemed to be staring at her from across the room, as if it were judging her, as if it were reading her very thoughts.

- The rabbit hopped across the road in front of him, causing him to swerve madly to the left. As he careered over the cliff, his life flashed in front of his eyes. It was so boring he had to laugh.

- The woman staring out of the photo seemed to be looking right at him, looking through his very soul. He had to find out who she was, and he had to do it today.

- Roger threw the crumpled newspaper across the

room. They always got it wrong, of course, but this time… this time they'd gone too far.

- As he waved his flag patriotically in the crowd, shouts reached his ears from across the courtyard. No, not shouts – screams.
- The house was falling apart around her and there was nothing she could do. Sitting down on the only chair left, she began to cry.

Questions To Answer In A Story

Come up with as weird an answer to one of these questions as you can, then see if any ideas come to you for a short story to write around it:

- What would happen if all technology broke for a month?
- What would happen if it stopped raining everywhere?
- What would happen if you woke up and your family had no idea who you were?
- What would happen if there was a chocolate shortage in the entire country?
- What would happen if the government folded in every single country?
- What would happen if you found out there was one person ruling the entire world?
- What would happen if animals suddenly started speaking English?

- What would happen if the dead started coming back to life (non-zombies)?
- What would happen if you found your way to an alternate dimension?
- What would happen if you started being able to hear everyone's thoughts?
- What would happen if an earthquake hit your town and devastated the whole area?
- What would happen if plants suddenly came to life?
- What would happen if you switched bodies with someone for a day?
- What would happen if your place of work received a bomb threat?
- What would happen if you suddenly forgot your entire childhood?
- What would happen if you developed a hundred phobias in a day?
- What would happen if you got addicted to dancing?
- What would happen if you found you couldn't physically look away from your computer screen?
- What would happen if you suddenly realised what the meaning of life was?
- What would happen if you started craving the most bizarre foods in the world?

Themes/Ideas To Explore In A Story

Take one of these themes (or more) and try and come up with a story to base around it.

- When power goes to a person's head.
- Do we rely too much on technology?
- What if love isn't enough?
- Fighting for freedom.
- Coming of age/the difficulties of growing up.
- Becoming isolated, both physically and psychologically.
- Injustice/Truth vs. Justice.
- Fear of death and how to conquer it.
- Going into survival mode.
- Manipulation and control.
- When jealousy takes hold of someone.
- Good vs. Evil, in all its forms.
- Chasing your dreams.
- Identity – what it means and how to find yours.
- The breakdown of a relationship.
- The lengths someone would go to in order to protect their family.
- Doing the wrong things for good reasons.
- Getting revenge.
- Insanity – how do we know when we're going insane?
- Nature vs. Nurture.

The Alphabet Of Short Stories

You may think that you're completely out of ideas, even for short stories and small writing exercises to get you in the creative zone. When I think this, I do a little thing involving the alphabet: I come up with a word or phrase for each letter, and once I've gone from A-Z, I look down the list and see if there's anything that stands out to me. Then I write about that thing, whatever it may be (and sometimes, it's pretty weird). Here's an alphabet example to get you started:

A. Aliens
B. Broken doll
C. Car won't start
D. Dead quiet
E. Evil family member
F. Ferry
G. Grocers at night
H. Hospital is empty
I. Internet goes wrong
J. Jewel with powers
K. Killer kitchen
L. Loser gets even
M. Monopoly game goes wrong
N. No one can hear you
O. Overgrown maze in a park
P. Possessed toy

Q. Queen bee

R. Rogue snake

S. Strange smells

T. Traffic problem

U. Umbrella shortage

V. Vines going crazy

W. Wine overload

X. X-ray shows something unexpected

Y. Year of danger

Z. Zimmer frame malfunction

Character Prompts

Creating characters – especially secondary characters who may not be in your story/novel much – can be difficult for some people. How do you make them different enough to everyone else? How do you make them interesting when they're not around for that long? If they're going to pop up again later, how do you ensure your readers will remember who they are? It's certainly tricky, but spending some time with some character prompts can help. Just take one or two of the following and build up a character around the details given. More of this can be seen in the 'World Building Cheat Sheets' section of the appendix, but here are some ideas to get you started for now:

- Kieran Flanagan. A middle-aged Irish pub owner who's arrived in London to open up his own Irish bar. Tall, slim, and with dark curly hair, he's a hit with all the ladies.

- Dorothy Turner. A seventy-year-old retired nurse, she still helps out in her local community when she can, and she often visits her older neighbours who can't get out much anymore.

- Lisa Hatwell. A young, pretty blonde woman who knows how to use her looks to get what she wants. She's ruthless, cunning, but has a heart underneath her ice cold facade - it can just be pretty hard to find it.

- Johnny Willis. A fifty-year-old ex-con who's been toughened up by life in prison. Very mysterious and quiet, no one knows what he was in for.

- Jeremy Higgins. A friendly yet slightly bizarre thirty-something who seems to pop up all over the town. He lives on his own with his dog, and never seems to work or do anything to earn money. No one knows much about him, despite his constant presence.

Why not give it a go now? See what stories you can come up with using those beginnings – they might take you in directions you didn't even think of to start with, and who knows? They could end up giving you ideas for a story of your own that you want to develop further.

If you've caught the writing prompt bug, how about checking out these websites and books for more ideas?

These are also listed in the Resources section of the appendix:

StoryADay - storyaday.org/category/inspiration/writing-prompts
Write Anything – Fiction Friday - writeanything.wordpress.com/fiction-friday
Creative Writing Prompts - www.creativewritingprompts.com
Writing Exercises & Prompts - writingexercises.co.uk
Book: 1,000 Creative Writing Prompts for Seasons
Book: 1,000 Awesome Writing Prompts
Book: 1,001 Writing Prompts for Generating Ideas
Book: 642 Things to Write
Book: 365 Journal Writing Ideas

Literary Socialising

Aspects of socialising have been mentioned elsewhere in these books, but there are several ideas I want to make sure I get in here, as writing is well known as being a lonely profession, and if you don't get out there and mingle with actual, real people every so often, you may find yourself in a bit of a rut and a bit of a literary pickle. Here are some other things you can do to socialise involving your love of literature.

Book Clubs

There are many reasons to join a local book club: the social aspect, expanding your reading list, the love of discussing literature, the food and wine (if it's that kind of book club), and there's also the motivation aspect. Seeing how others view and discuss books can give you different perspectives you might not otherwise have been aware of, and it may allow you to think about your own storylines and characters in a different light as well. It's a good way of getting out the house once a month (or every few weeks, or however long your book club gives you to read a novel) if you work from home, and if you're in the habit of sticking to the same old genre when it comes to your reading pile, it will help you break that habit spectacularly; book clubs usually read a variety of novels – both classic and contemporary – and it's a great way of fuelling your love of reading in a different, more social way (especially as reading is a pretty solitary activity!).

Take a look online to see where your local meetings are, or suggest starting a book club within your group of friends. Take it in turn to go to each other's houses to host, and add in some nibbles and drinks (tea is just as good as wine) to make it more of an occasion. If you often make the excuse that you 'don't have time' to read, this will make you do it, but if you don't have time to read, do you really have time to be a writer? It's worth asking the question, and then picking up a book.

Literary Festivals, Writing Workshops And Other Writing Events

Fans of both reading and writing can find great inspiration at literary festivals, which take place up and down the country throughout the year. You can find out about new releases, talk to other writers, and even meet and hear talks given by famous authors. It's bound to be inspiring, and you might come away with some great ideas and the desire to sit down and write, write, write! These are generally open to everyone, and they range in scale and format.

If you make the most of the festival you go to – hearing as many speakers as you can, mingling with other writers (and readers) and generally just soaking up as much of the atmosphere (and as much knowledge) as humanly possibly, you can't really *not* come away feeling inspired, motivated and pumped to get going with your own work. This is procrastiworking at its finest, mixed as it is with networking and learning, and just by attending a literary festival you'll start to feel part of a community, part of something special – somewhere you (and all your crazy writing ideas) belong. How can that be a bad thing?

Check out these websites to find out if there are any literary festivals near you (please note, I'm focusing mainly on UK literary festivals here, although they're held all over the world). These links are also listed in the Resources section of the appendix:

Literary Festivals - www.literaryfestivals.co.uk
British Council – Literature - literature.britishcouncil.org/festivals
The World Travels Literary Festivals In The UK - www.thewordtravels.com/literary-festivals.html
The Telegraph – World's Best Book Festivals - www.telegraph.co.uk/travel/picturegalleries/9455946/The-worlds-best-book-festivals.html
London Literature Festival - www.southbankcentre.co.uk/whatson/festivals-series/london-literature-festival
Manchester Literature Festival - www.manchesterliteraturefestival.co.uk
Manchester Children's Book Festival - www.mcbf.org.uk
Bath Literature Festival - bathfestivals.org.uk/literature
Stratford-upon-Avon Literature Festival - www.stratfordliteraryfestival.co.uk
Hay Festival - www.hayfestival.com/portal/index.aspx?skinid=1&localesetting=en-GB

There are also a whole load of writers' workshops and networking events that take place all over the country. These can often be a little pricey, but you're bound to come away with a lot of knowledge and a whole heap of inspiration as well. Add to this all the courses and classes out there, and you're surrounded with many, many options if you're looking for some new writing knowledge. Pages at the <u>Writers & Artists</u> and <u>The Writers' Workshop</u> websites are great resources.

Get A Mentor

Getting to know as many writers as you can will give you a lot of knowledge and a lot of people to ask for advice, but sometimes that can all get a little too much, especially if you're trying to keep up with them all on various social media sites and if you're constantly trying to read all their latest releases. One way to get around this is to find an author who's been writing for some time, and preferably in the genre or area you want to write in (although this isn't absolutely necessary). As long as they're OK with it, of course, you can treat this writer as your kind of mentor, as authors generally like helping others to achieve what they've already achieved, and it's often mutually beneficial if you both enjoy reading each other's work. Getting advice from people who have been through it all can be much more useful that doing a simple web search, and you'll probably find yourself learning much more than you thought you would.

When The End Is In Sight

Now, most of these books have been focused on how we get into the creative zone in the first place (as they should be, going by their titles..!) but I thought it was worth adding in a few little sections about what to do when you're coming towards the end of your novel. When do you start showing people? What happens if you get bad reviews? And what are you going to do now?!

Writing Drafts And When To Let Them Go

This is going to be different for each individual writer, but in my case, I don't let a manuscript out of my sight until I've finished several drafts of it and are more or less happy with how it reads. I would never, ever let anyone see my first draft, mainly because I vomit words onto the page during my first draft and so it would probably not even be readable for most people, but also because my story usually changes so much between drafts. With my first novel, *The Former World*, I really didn't know what I was doing, and what started out as a 60,000 word straightforward crime/whodunit novel actually turned into a 130,000 word paranormal mystery novel.

If anyone had read my first draft before I started tweaking the story, they probably would have tried to discourage me from my writing, which is never something any writer wants, no matter what their ability and no matter how far along in the writing process they are. Of course, some people show their writing at every stage, getting feedback on what works and what doesn't, and if that works for you – great. You're braver than I am. It can be really hard to let your project loose on the world (or even a few people to start with) but just remember: this is why you wanted to be a writer. What would be the point of writing if you only wrote for yourself? You already know the story, you wrote it! So although it feels like baring your soul to the world (which, it pretty much is), this is what you've been working towards. So don't think about it too much – just do it – and let the idea of people actually reading your draft motivate you to get it finished.

Ignoring Bad Reviews

Bad reviews. All writers get them, no matter how good you are, because not every reader thinks the same, or likes the same stuff. People have different tastes and styles, and what may be amazing to one person isn't going to be someone else's cup of tea at all. Not only this, but it depends on what your readers are expecting to read. Before I rebranded my Little Forest books, I got complaints because some readers didn't realise they were – arguably – Young Adult books (although I've had plenty of adults of all ages who've liked them). Because of this, they were expecting something else, and their bad review reflected this misunderstanding more than anything else. So, make sure you're clear about the type and genre of book you have (and if you're not sure, ask a few people to read it and let you know what they think), and get a thick skin, as soon as you possibly can.

You will get bad reviews, so just be prepared, and don't get depressed or disheartened when you read them. Unless they give good constructive criticism, read them once and then forget about them, and whatever you do, don't reply to them; don't get into a meaningless argument with someone online who is never going to change their opinion, as it makes you look bad and it can put other people off reading your book at all. Bad reviews are bad, but not having any bad reviews on your Amazon listing can be even worse – if you've got fifty five-star reviews all saying the same thing, people will assume you got your friends and family members to write them all, whether you did or not. A range of different ratings on a book's page can actually encourage some people to buy it, as it looks like a 'real' listing. You can't please everyone – something we all know in our everyday lives, but something we often forget about when it comes to our own work. Of course, it's very personal and our books are often our babies, but you just have to learn to let it go.

Careers

You may be getting into writing as a hobby, which is great, but if you're good at it, why not pursue it as a career? Or at least use your skills to earn some extra cash around your normal job? Even if you only want to write novels, it's worth having a think about other ways to make money with your writing – and think outside the box too. All kinds of businesses rely on writers in one way or another, and you might end up somewhere a little unexpected. There's just so much you can do with writing, and thinking about them all can be great motivation to hone your craft:

- Writing fiction books, novels and short stories
- Writing poetry
- Writing non-fiction
- Screenplay writing for films
- Writing for TV
- Writing for theatre
- Copywriting, content writing, writing online blogs and articles for business
- Being a Journalist
- Freelance writing for local publications
- Editing and proofreading
- Ghostwriting
- Writing for games
- Writing speeches
- Writing tours for tour guides and other similar entertainment style scripts
- Writing kid's books and for kid's TV
- Songwriting
- Writing for documentaries/scripts/research
- Writing press releases and other marketing copy

Just think of all the possibilities for both your career and your hobbies, and then get writing. You never know where your writing will take you, and that's one of the most exciting things about it. Once you've mastered how to get into that creative zone quickly and easily (with whichever techniques work for you), the world is pretty much going to be your oyster.

So what are you waiting for? Write! Write! Write!

Conclusion

There are many more ways to start writing your book, but the message here is: think outside the box, outside the word processor, outside the computer. Laptops are our friends when it comes to getting our first draft down on virtual paper, but they can also be our enemies, sucking out our creativity and turning the act of writing into something daunting and overwhelming.

I realise that not every idea in these books will be for everyone, but on some level, that's the point –maybe you're stuck in your writing rut because you haven't been trying anything new, no matter how silly or strange an idea it may seem. You need to get out of your comfort zone, go and do something you've never done before, and gain experience in how to reset your brain and get it into that zone of creativity as quickly as you can. By allowing your brain to be creative in the way it wants to do it, you may well start seeing some new and exciting results.

I really hope you've enjoyed reading this book and that it's at least given you some inspiration to go and get writing, or carry on writing, or finish the writing you've been trying to get done. If you've used some of the ideas and techniques in these volumes and they've worked, let me know! I love to get feedback from readers, as well as other writers, and maybe I can learn from you like you've (hopefully) learnt something from these books.

Just email me at author@jessicagracecoleman.com.

Anyone can sit down and try and write something, but if you take the time to get in the right headspace, you can sit down and write something worth reading. Get rid of that self-doubt, knock down that creative block, and start following your passion. Grab yourself some inspiration, believe in yourself, and get writing!

Appendix

Resources
Easy To Read List Of Creative Techniques
Writing Prompts
Writing Quotes
Creative Playlists
World Building Cheat Sheets
Literary Tourism Travel Plan
Your Writing Wall
Blog Examples

Resources

There are many more ways to start writing your book, but the message here is: think outside the box, outside the word processor, outside the computer.

The following are all of the websites, apps and computer programs mentioned in this book. Again, I am not being paid to recommend any of these, they are simply things I have used – or think would be useful – to get you into the creative writing mindset. They are listed by category, and most links are to UK sites.

A special mention goes to the book cover designer for the Creative Ways Series:

James from GoOnWrite.com

Self-Publishing vs. Traditional Publishing

The Write Life Self-Publishing vs. Traditional Infographic - thewritelife.com/se
Scribendi Traditional Publishing vs. Self-publishing - www.scribendi.com/advice/traditional_versus_self_publ ishing.en.html

Miami Herald 'Self-publishing vs. traditional publishing: How to choose?' - www.miamiherald.com/news/business/biz-monday/article3950085.html

Jane Friedman – Self-Publish or Perish - janefriedman.com/leap-to-indie/

The Guardian 'Traditional publishing is 'no longer fair or sustainable', says Society of Authors - www.theguardian.com/books/2014/jul/11/traditional-publishing-fair-sustainable-society-of-authors

Self-Publish Or Not - http://www.underdown.org/self-publish.htm

Nielsen: Self-Publishing Now More Like Traditional Publishing - publishingperspectives.com/2015/06/nielsen-self-publishing-now-more-like-traditional-publishing/

Self-Publishing Websites

Amazon Kindle Direct Publishing - kdp.amazon.com
Createspace - www.createspace.com
Lightning Source - www.lightningsource.com
IngramSpark - www.ingramspark.com
Smashwords - www.smashwords.com
Nielsen (UK ISBN Agency) - www.isbn.nielsenbook.co.uk/controller.php?page=121
Writers & Artists - www.writersandartists.co.uk

Stock Photo Websites

Fotolia - en.fotolia.com
Shutterstock - www.shutterstock.com
iStock - www.istockphoto.com
Bigstock - www.bigstockphoto.com
Getty Images - www.gettyimages.co.uk

Book Covers (Premade and Bespoke)

GoOnWrite - www.goonwrite.com
Creative Paramita - http://www.creativeparamita.com
The Book Cover Designer -
www.thebookcoverdesigner.com
The Cover Collection - www.thecovercollection.com
Tanya Back Designs - www.tanyaback.com
Ebook Indie Covers - ebookindiecovers.com
The Book Cover Machine -
bookcovermachine.wordpress.com
Spiffing Covers - www.spiffingcovers.com
The Book Cover Archive - bookcoverarchive.com
Bespoke Book Covers - bespokebookcovers.com

Font Websites

Font Squirrel - www.fontsquirrel.com
DaFont - www.dafont.com
Lost Type - www.losttype.com
The League of Moveable Type -
www.theleagueofmoveabletype.com
Font Monger - www.fontmonger.com

Inspirational Writing And Other Quotes

Goodreads.com
Brainyquote.com
Writersdigest.com
Keepinspiring.me
Inspirational-quotes.info

Writer Resources

Kboards - www.kboards.com
The Creative Penn - www.thecreativepenn.com
The Self-Publishing Podcast -
selfpublishingpodcast.com
Writer's Beat - www.writersbeat.com
Absolute Write - www.absolutewrite.com
Alliance of Independent Authors -
allianceindependentauthors.org
Writing Excuses Podcast -
http://www.writingexcuses.com
Grammar Girl - www.quickanddirtytips.com/grammar-
girl
Positive Writer - positivewriter.com

Writer Interviews

Stephen King Powell's interview -
www.powells.com/blog/interviews/the-once-and-future-
stephen-king-by-jill/
JK Rowling Amazon interview -
www.amazon.com/gp/feature.html?docId=6230
Ian Rankin Writers & Artists interview -
www.writersandartists.co.uk/writers/advice/39/a-
writers-toolkit/interviews-with-authors/interview-with-
ian-rankin
Terry Pratchett The Telegraph interview -
www.telegraph.co.uk/culture/books/authorinterviews/10
396286/Terry-Pratchett-interview-a-fantasy-writer-
facing-reality.html
Neil Gaiman New Republic interview -
www.newrepublic.com/article/115682/neil-gaiman-
interview
Toni Morrison Goodreads interview -
www.goodreads.com/interviews/show/1029.Toni_Morri
son

Dan Brown BookBrowse interview -
www.bookbrowse.com/author_interviews/full/index.cf
m?author_number=226
Janet Evanovich Internet Writing Journal interview -
http://www.writerswrite.com/journal/jan99/a-
conversation-with-janet-evanovich-1991
Chuck Palahniuk DVD Talk interview -
www.dvdtalk.com/interviews/chuck_palahniuk.html

Books On Writing

On Writing: A Memoir of the Craft by Stephen King
Zen in the Art of Writing by Ray Bradbury
The War of Art by Steven Pressfield
Writing Down the Bones: Feeling the Writer Within by
Natalie Goldberg
The Writing Life by Annie Dillard
How to Write Bestselling Fiction by Dean Koontz
The Elements of Style by William Strunk Jr. and E.B.
White

Service Websites

Fiverr - fiverr.com
FiverUp - fiverup.com
GigBucks - gigbucks.com

Ways To Write & Plot

Microsoft Word - www.microsoftstore.com
Scrivener - www.literatureandlatte.com
Final Draft - www.finaldraft.com
Write Or Die - writeordie.com
Apple Pages - www.apple.com/uk/mac/pages/
HanxWriter - www.hitcents.com/b2b/work/hanx

Werdsmith - werdsmith.com
IndexCard - www.denvog.com/app/index-card/
StorySkeleton - www.storyskeleton.com
Story Planner for Writers - www.literautas.com/en/apps/story-planner-for-writers-app-outline-your-novel/
Word Keeper - www.preapps.com/new-iphone-ipad-apps/word-keeper-track-writing-progress-with-timer-charts-and-stats-for-author-writer-and-student/3034
Microsoft Excel - www.microsoftstore.com
Evernote - www.evernote.com

Concentration Tools

SnoreStore.co.uk (Earplugs)
Spotify.com (Music)

Writers' Groups – Online and In Person

Write Words Writers' Groups - www.writewords.org.uk/groups
Great Writing - www.greatwriting.co.uk
UK Writers' College List of Writing Circles in the UK - www.ukwriterscollege.co.uk/Writing+Resources/UK+Writers+College++Writing+Circles.html
Writers Online List of Writing Groups - www.writers-online.co.uk/Writers-Groups/
Scribeophile Writing Group - www.scribophile.com
Facebook - www.facebook.com
Streetlife - www.streetlife.com
Meetup - www.meetup.com

Online Writing Courses

Groupon - www.groupon.co.uk

Oxford University Continuing Education – Online & Distance Learning - http://www.ox.ac.uk/admissions/continuing-education/online-and-distance-courses
ALISON - alison.com
FutureLearn - www.futurelearn.com
The Writers' Workshop - www.writersworkshop.co.uk
UEA Creative Writing Online Courses - https://www.uea.ac.uk/literature/creative-writing/creative-writing-online

Crowdfunding

Kickstarter - www.kickstarter.com
Indiegogo - www.indiegogo.com
Rockethub - www.rockethub.com
GoGetFunding - gogetfunding.com
FundRazr - www.fundrazr.com
Crowdrise - www.crowdrise.com
GoFundMe - www.gofundme.com
Crowdfunder - www.crowdfunder.co.uk

Website Hosting / Building

Wix - www.wix.com
WordPress - wordpress.com
GoDaddy - www.godaddy.com
1and1 - www.1and1.co.uk
Moonfruit - www.moonfruit.com
Ehost - www.ehost.com
HostClear - www.hostclear.com
Idea Host - www.ideahost.com
Weebly - www.weebly.com
Website Builder - www.websitebuilder.com

Travel

Google Images - images.google.com
Google Maps - maps.google.co.uk
YouTube - www.youtube.com
Voice Record Pro -
www.bejbej.info/app/voicerecordpro
Smart Voice Recorder - recorder.smartmobdev.com

Writing Retreats

The Watermill, Italy - www.watermill.net
Moniack Mhor, Scotland - www.moniackmhor.org.uk
Urban Writers' Retreat, Devon -
http://www.urbanwritersretreat.co.uk/a-residential-
writing-retreat/
Annie McKie Retreats, Writing and Communication
Services - www.anniemckie.co.uk
The Grange, short breaks by the sea -
www.thegrangebythesea.com

Naming Your Characters

BabyNames.co.uk
The Guardian – 100 Most Popular Baby Names 2014 -
www.theguardian.com/news/datablog/ng-
interactive/2015/aug/17/100-most-popular-baby-names-
england-wales-full-list
BabyNames.com
BabyNames.org.uk
Baby Center – Popular Baby Names For US By Year -
www.babycenter.com
Behind The Name – History Names -
www.behindthename.com/names/usage/history
Behind The Name – English Surnames -

surnames.behindthename.com/names/usage/english
Name Nerds – Irish Names - www.namenerds.com/irish
European Baby Names And Meanings -
babynames.allparenting.com/babynames/Tips/European
_Baby_Names_and_Meanings/
Popular Norse Names - babynames.net/all/old-norse

Adult Colouring Books

Millie Marotta's Animal Kingdom – A Colouring Book Adventure by Millie Marotta
Secret Garden: An Inky Treasure Hunt and Colouring Book by Johanna Basford
The Mindfulness Colouring Book: Anti-stress art therapy for busy people by Emma Farrarons
The Art Therapy Colouring Book by Richard Merritt and Hannah Davies
The Can't Sleep Colouring Book (Creative Colouring for Grown-Ups) by Various
Colour Therapy (Creative Colouring for Grown-Ups) by Cindy Wilde and Laura-Kate Chapman
Japanese Patterns (Creative Colouring for Grown-Ups) by Various Authors

Fanfic

FanFiction.Net
Quotev - www.quotev.com
Kindle Worlds - kindleworlds.amazon.com
Feedbooks - www.feedbooks.com
Wattpad - www.wattpad.com

Blog Sites

Blogger - www.blogger.com

WordPress - www.wordpress.com
SquareSpace - www.squarespace.com
Tumblr - www.tumblr.com
Google+ - plus.google.com
Hubpages - www.hubpages.com
Medium - www.medium.com
Live Journal - www.livejournal.com
Joomla - www.joomla.org
Typepad - www.typepad.com

Writing Prompts Websites & Books

StoryADay - storyaday.org/category/inspiration/writing-prompts
Write Anything – Fiction Friday - writeanything.wordpress.com/fiction-friday
Creative Writing Prompts - www.creativewritingprompts.com
Writing Exercises & Prompts - writingexercises.co.uk
Book: 1,000 Creative Writing Prompts for Seasons
Book: 1,000 Awesome Writing Prompts
Book: 1,001 Writing Prompts for Generating Ideas
Book: 642 Things to Write
Book: 365 Journal Writing Ideas

Literary Festivals, Writing Workshops And Other Writing Events

Literary Festivals - www.literaryfestivals.co.uk
British Council – Literature - literature.britishcouncil.org/festivals
The World Travels Literary Festivals In The UK - www.thewordtravels.com/literary-festivals.html
The Telegraph – World's Best Book Festivals - www.telegraph.co.uk/travel/picturegalleries/9455946/T

he-worlds-best-book-festivals.html
London Literature Festival -
www.southbankcentre.co.uk/whatson/festivals-
series/london-literature-festival
Manchester Literature Festival -
www.manchesterliteraturefestival.co.uk
Manchester Children's Book Festival -
www.mcbf.org.uk
Bath Literature Festival - bathfestivals.org.uk/literature
Stratford-upon-Avon Literature Festival -
www.stratfordliteraryfestival.co.uk
Hay Festival -
www.hayfestival.com/portal/index.aspx?skinid=1&local
esetting=en-GB

Other Apps

Name Dice - thinkamingo.com/name-dice
Lists For Writers - itunes.apple.com/gb/app/lists-for-
writers-ideas-for/id506577862?mt=8
Pinterest - www.pinterest.com
Noteshelf - www.noteshelf.net
Fifty Three - www.fiftythree.com
Moleskine Journal -
www.moleskine.com/microsites/apps

Dictation

Apple Pages - www.apple.com/uk/mac/pages
Dragon Dictation - www.nuance.co.uk/for-
individuals/mobile-applications/dragon-
dictation/index.htm
Microsoft Word - www.nuance.co.uk/for-
individuals/mobile-applications/dragon-
dictation/index.htm

Jessica Grace Coleman

My Own Books

The Former World – Little Forest Book One
Memento Mori – Little Forest Book Two
The Exalted – Little Forest Book Three
Carnival Masquerade – Little Forest Book Four
The Gloaming – Little Forest Book Five
Little Forest Series Box Set Novels 1-4
Grown By The Wicked Moon (Short Story Collection)
Creative Ways To Start Creative Writing Volume One
Creative Ways To Start Creative Writing Volume Two
Creative Ways To Start Creative Writing Volume Three

My Websites

JessicaGraceColeman.com
ColemanEditing.co.uk
Author Facebook Page -
www.facebook.com/JessicaGraceColeman
Author Twitter Page -
www.twitter.com/jessformerworld
Author Email - author@jessicagracecoleman.com

Easy To Read List Of Creative Techniques

I thought I'd list the basic ideas here from this book, written separately and without the other writing around it, so you can have a quick look to see which exercise or technique you might want to try next. Please just read the actual books first – out of context, some of these ideas may seem even crazier than they did to me when I started planning these books!

Creative Ways To Start Creative Writing, Volume One

- Visualise the result you want: holding that finished book in your hands, getting your first royalty cheque from online sales, showing your family and friends your completed novel. Hey, why not go even bigger? Visualise yourself living the life you want: writing, and making money from it. How great would it feel to wake up every morning knowing that your job is to write novels? Keep that in mind throughout your writing and work towards it. Visualise it every day if it helps, or every time you get stuck with your book.

- Learn how to procrastiwork! Now, in a way, many of the ideas and techniques listed in these books can come under the category of procrastiworking, which is basically procrastination but with a point – working on something but not necessarily the large project you should be working on. Procrastiworking can include doing research, reading, planning, looking up writer resources and interviews, and creating your author website.

- Ignore other people. That's right: if they're being negative or doubtful about your ability to write a book, or if they have their own opinion about what makes a great novel that aren't helpful to you whatsoever, just ignore them. They're not the one writing a book, and the last thing you need is people putting doubts in your head if you already have some of your own. Learning to ignore others – especially if they're a family member or close friend – can be hard, but it'll be worth it when you present them with your finished book.

- Learn how to deal with people's reactions – both negative and positive. When you tell your friends and family you're writing a book, some might have an attitude of 'I'll believe that when I see it' whereas others might be so excited they'll keep asking you about it at every chance they get. Both reactions can be a little overwhelming, but turn your response into something positive. Show them that you can do it, and also use the friend who's constantly asking for updates as a reason to write so many words each day. Then thank them in your

252

acknowledgments for keeping you writing!

- Think about the money! As a writer, you're probably not in this for the money, but wouldn't it be nice to think you could earn some pennies from it? Visualise those royalty cheques and get motivated. Even if you end up earning just a few pounds a month, making money from your own books is a great feeling, and knowing that people are actually reading your words can be even better!

- Research, research, research. You might not need to do a lot of research for your book, but even little things can be made more realistic in your novel if you know more about them (for example, if one of your characters is reporting a crime, but you've never done that or even been in a police station). This is great for procrastiworking if you're not ready to start writing yet, and the more knowledge you have, the more realistic your work will be.

- Get some self-belief: repeat mantras, think of those people you want to prove right (or wrong), read some inspirational, motivational self-help books if you're into that, and get positive. Get rid of any doubts, and start getting excited. Just believe in yourself. You can do this.

- Research how you're going to try and publish your book – traditional/self-publishing etc, but don't get too hung up on this. Knowing what you're aiming for can help you visualise the finished thing, and anyway, knowledge is power. The more you know about writing, the more interest you'll have in getting your book written.

- Plot and plan your book using a wide range of

different techniques, from getting crafty with a scrapbook to going all crazy-detective with pin boards, images and maps. Post-it all your scenes or use the cork board on Scrivener to get your head around everything. There are so many different ways you can get planning – it doesn't have to be as boring as simply typing words onto a blank page.

- Create a PowerPoint presentation about your book, laying out the main plots, introducing the characters, and illustrating how your book is going to stand out from the crowd. Do it as if you're doing a presentation at school or work – it might get you thinking about your writing differently, and if you regularly do these sorts of presentations for your job, you might find it easier than sitting and staring at a blank word document.

- Use a large artist's sketchbook to plan your novel, using it like a flip chart. Thick, different coloured markers can be used for different parts of your novel, and getting away from the screen or a small notepad you usually use can make you think about your plot differently. It's all about changing things up until you find what works for you.

- Get world building! If you're writing about a fictional place, this is definitely something you'll need to do anyway, and the good news is that it can be really fun. You get to create entire worlds – how many other professions can claim that? Get creative when planning your fictional towns and cities, and look at the World Building Cheat Sheets section of the appendix for more ideas on how to start.

- Get covered! Even if you're not going to self-publish, getting a premade cover can really help you start to visualise that finished outcome. Head online and look at premade covers until you find one you like, or commission someone to design a cover for you. Hell, even design one yourself if you have the tools and the skills. Print it out and put it on your wall next to where you work – it's a brilliant motivator.

- Even if you don't get to the finished cover part, take a look at images online (using stock photo websites) and fonts, and imagine what your cover is going to look like. Sometimes just looking through images (and other book covers in the genre you're writing in) can be enough to inspire you.

- Search for and read as many writing quotes (and general inspirational quotes) as you can – those featured in the book can be found in their own section in the appendix. Print some out and stick them around your writing room, or keep them in an easy to access folder on your desktop for when you need some quick inspiration.

Creative Ways To Start Creative Writing, Volume Two

- Read as many writer interviews and resources as you can. Knowledge is power, and if you do decide to self-publish, finding out about the industry as you write your book will really help you when you get to the point of actually publishing it – it won't seem as daunting if you've done your homework. Plus, reading about other writers' successes is a great motivator.

- Read books on writing as well, such as Stephen King's *On Writing: A Memoir Of The Craft*. Get into the headspace of a writer.

- Get inspiration from service websites such as Fiverr. Look at what they're offering in terms of book covers, writing help, marketing help, and other fun things, and see what you can do to help yourself with your book – and for a bargain price too.

- Try out different ways to actually write your book, from a word processor to Scrivener, Final Draft to Write or Die, and even tablets, typewriters, and the good old-fashioned notebook and pen. Trying different things – and in different settings – might be what you need to change your current mindset and get into the creative zone.

- Use dictation programs. Do your fingers get tired of typing? Do you get headaches from concentrating on the screen so much? Take a break and use some dictation software to help you get those initial words on (virtual) paper. It'll give your hands a rest, but don't rely on it for anything other than notes or a first draft – the mistakes can be annoying, but pretty hilarious sometimes.

- Learn how to concentrate and forget about the world around you while you work! Invest in some high quality earplugs, relax with a nice, soothing tea, find a good writing space, and listen to some music that's perfect for concentration (check out the playlists section of the appendix if you need help locating some of these tracks). Create your own little writing nest and write. If you do the same things to prepare for your writing every time, your brain will start to recognise the routine and will (hopefully) get ready to work.

- If writing a full blown story is too daunting, start with a short story. If that's too daunting, start with flash fiction. Or perhaps try a poem, or a haiku. When you're first starting out, it doesn't matter what you're writing as long as you're writing something regularly. Plus, who knows? One of those haikus or short stories could be the beginning of a novel or series. You just need to start somewhere.

- Read books by your favourite author to get into the write headspace, and books from the genre you're planning on writing in can help as well – just don't start gleaning ideas from specific novels!

- Join writing groups both online and in person. Get to know other writers and get feedback on your work – win win. Networking with other authors on sites such as Facebook and Twitter can also be great – a brilliant way to 'procrastiwork'.

- As with joining writers' groups online and in person, if you work from home it can be useful to join any sort of group that meets up locally, to get out the house and give yourself a break from the computer screen. There are particular groups up and down the country for people who work from home, so have a search.

- Take a writing course either online or in person.

There are loads to choose from, from intros to creative writing to more advanced, more specific courses on particular genres. It works better if you have classmates (either real life or virtual), so if you're doing one online, look for ones with their own forums and message boards where you can interact with the teacher and with the others taking the course. This way you can learn both from the syllabus and from each other.

- Get playing games and socialising online. Sometimes, you just need to switch your writing brain off for a bit and do something else, and a quick game involving logical thinking with another person will fill up your social quota a bit and get your brain working on something else for a few minutes. With the break, you might find that when you get back to your writing, your plot hole has been filled in or that problem with the character has been sorted out when you weren't even paying attention. I love it when that happens.

- Check out several crowdfunding sites, both for inspiration and as a possible way of raising some money yourself. Look at how authors have used these sites to get their books self-published, and while you're there, why not sign up and put a few pounds towards helping out a literary (or other) project? You might get your name mentioned in a book, and it's nice to feel a part of something and see how a project grows over the weeks and months.

- Create your official author website. You can pay someone to do this, of course, but I find that the act of creating your site yourself can really help get you motivated – just imagine all the titles that are going to be listed under your 'Books' page! Giving your future fans a place to come and learn all about you (other than on your social media profiles) is vital.

- Relax! Especially if you're working to a (self-imposed or otherwise) deadline, it can be difficult to step away from the computer and take some time out for yourself, but your brain and your body won't thank you if you do too much work and burn out. Have a bath, have a glass of wine, listen to some music, light some candles… just take some time to switch your brain off completely. Try some meditation or go for a walk. The break will do you good, and when you get back to writing, you might find you have better concentration and more motivation than ever.

- Clear your mind through activity. Just like relaxing or going on holiday, exercise can be a great way of giving your mind a break for an hour or two, especially if you do your exercise outside in the fresh air. Clear your head as you feel those endorphins rushing around your body, and use that energy to come back and write.

- Clear your head through other activities such as driving (but don't clear it so much that you forget how to drive… that would be bad). If you can drive in the country somewhere with less traffic and nice surroundings, you can really let your mind reset itself. Another way of achieving this is to drive using computer games, like racing games or a certain game that allows you to steal cars and take part in dodgy activities… It sounds a little weird, but just clear your head as you drive around, or use the time to think about your writing as you go. It will work for some people, but others may just get caught up in the idea of car chases and illegal activities in the game (which, if you're writing about criminals, could come in handy anyway!). Think like a criminal, then write like a criminal. Just don't go around acting like a criminal – 'book research' will only get you so far as a defence.

- In a similar vein, take a holiday to get away from your writing, even if it's just for a few days. It doesn't have to be anywhere exotic, and if you really can't afford the money or the time, just a day trip to a local spa or a place in the country can be enough to reset your overworked brain. Take this idea even further and look into Literary Tourism – the Travel Plan in the appendix should give you some places to start.

- Book yourself on a writer's retreat, whether it's one with workshops and other writers, or just one where you can go on your own, sit in a lovely room with a lovely view, and have no other responsibilities for a few days other than writing. Choose one in a nice location and add a daily walk into your routine to help you mull over storylines. It's a great way of having a bit of a break, but also getting a lot of work done, and if you're paying for the privilege, you won't want to come back without having written any words!

- Have fun with names. Naming your characters can be an interesting job, but when you have so many, it can be difficult to keep coming up with new – and different – ideas. Make it more fun by giving them names that reflect their personality, or use an app to generate random first names and surnames for inspiration. Use baby name websites and look up the historical meanings for names from certain geographic regions or certain decades. Make your names mean something.

Creative Ways To Start Creative Writing, Volume Three

- Use music to get into the zone. I've mentioned music to help you concentrate, but other genres can also be used effectively when writing. Use motivational songs to get you pumped up to write, or listen to bands and artists that your protagonist would listen to, in order to get into their mindset. Creating playlists for your characters (and scenes) can be a fun thing to do as well. See the Creative Playlists section in the appendix for more ideas on this.
- Get in the creative zone by getting crafty. For instance, make a collage, using images of people and locations that have inspired you in your writing. Make pretty character profiles using different materials, or draw a detailed map of the town where your story is set. Use Pinterest and other similar sites for inspiration, or simply have a look on Google Images to find pictures you can use.
- If you're more creative in other ways, such as drawing, start sketching out your book ideas first – perhaps in the form of a three-panel comic. It's all about getting yourself into the creative headspace, no matter how you go about doing it.

- Scribble, doodle, and use adult colouring books. These are all great ways of getting the creative juices flowing without having to sit and type words that might not be coming quite as easily as you'd hoped. Drawing and painting will get you in the arty mood, and you may even draw something from your novel that will inspire you to get writing. And don't worry if you don't have an artistic bone in your body in terms of drawing, just doodle or invest in some adult colouring books. As long as you can keep in the lines, you can create some pretty magnificent works of art without having the ability to draw. Reset your brain with art and then head back to the writing afterwards.

- Take some inspiration from films and the theatre. Go and see a play, comparing the performance to the written words, or read a screenplay and then watch a film to see how the dialogue and action was transferred onto the screen. You could even write some scenes from your novel into a play or screenplay, and to make it even more fun, you can perform parts to your friends, getting them involved if there's more than one character in the scene. They can help give you feedback and you can see if your dialogue works or if it sounds clunky and wooden when said out loud.

- Write to your favourite author, telling them why you enjoy their work and how it has inspired you to write yourself. You'll probably have more luck with getting a response if you don't choose someone really famous, but even just the act of writing the letter or email can get you motivated.

Remember what you loved about writing and reading in the first place.

- As well as putting up writing quotes and future book covers on the wall above your writing desk, why not print infographics on writing and other images that will get you motivated? There are plenty online, so start browsing now. You can also put up flyers and business cards you've had made, any interviews you've done for local publications, or reviews of your previous books if you have any. Just something you can look at and get a quick boost of inspiration from.

- Take a few steps in your characters' shoes: if you're finding it difficult to get into the mind of a character, go and spend a day doing what they do. If they live in a city and hang out in coffee bars, do that. If they live in the country and a lot of the story takes place in a local pub, go and hang out in a local pub. You can legitimately call this 'research' and you also get a day out, away from your computer screen. Just use your common sense – if your character is a mass murderer, just stay at home.

- Think about your book dedication. This can really help with motivation, especially if you're writing the book for someone who has passed away – you'll want to get the book finished to honour their memory. If you're writing it for someone who's alive, let them know while you're still in the planning/writing stage. You won't want to let them down by not finishing your book, and just picturing yourself giving them a finished copy can be all the motivation you need.

- Try non-fiction. This book is primarily aimed at people who do creative writing, but sometimes, writing non-fiction can be a great way to get the writing juices flowing, without having to use your imagination quite so much. Write about what you've done this week, or start writing up bits of your childhood as if you were writing your memoirs. Just get words onto the paper, and who knows, you might end up using them in years to come when you actually do sit down and write your life story.

- Get gimmicky with non-fiction. Think about books like *Yes Man* by Danny Wallace and see if you can come up with something similar to do that you can then write about, whether it's for a book, a blog, or just as a writing exercise that may never see the light of day. Do something crazy or completely out of character, and then write about it in an interesting/funny/thoughtful way. Do it enough times and you might actually have enough material for a book!

- Keep a diary. Again, this is a way to get you writing every day (or as much as you can), and it's great practice, especially if you want to write non-fiction in the future. Don't just list what you did, where you went, and what you ate; write about how you felt that day, and what emotions passed through your body at various points in the week. Pick out something that made you stop, or smile, or feel sad, and discuss why – even if no one else reads it. As a bonus, if you do decide to write your life story when you're older, you'll have plenty of material to go on if you keep a diary every day.

- Take inspiration from your dreams. Keep a dream diary so you can write them down before they start to fade from your mind, and use the strange ramblings of your subconscious as potential ideas for future novels, even if it's just for a scene here or there. Dreams can be powerful, as well as absolutely insanely random, so make them a source of your writing!
- Hang out with friends. This can be a good 'mind resetting' activity, like relaxing in the bath or going for a walk, but you can also use a gathering of friends (and/or family members) as an opportunity to get feedback on your ideas. Offer them some wine and nibbles in exchange for their thoughts on your main characters, your location, your plot... everything. If you've made a crafty collage or scrapbook, show them that, and ask them how they'd react in certain situations – are your characters believable enough in their actions and reactions? Plus, it can just be a fun evening all round.
- If you're writing in the crime or mystery genres, why not try simplifying your plot and writing your own murder mystery script? Get some friends together and have fun acting out the scenes and becoming each character. You might get some useful feedback, but even if you don't, it'll be a fun activity to do using your own characters and plots.
- You don't have to start a novel from the start. Beginnings of stories can be notoriously difficult to write, especially if it's a brand new project or if you haven't been writing for long. So, if there's a scene further along in the book that

gets you excited (or that should get the reader excited), start with that and go back to the beginning afterwards. You can always change the details/add to it on the second draft, just get the words down on the page in the first instance, no matter what order you write the scenes in.

- Write what you know. It's a cliché but a cliché for a reason. Take events from your past and weave them into your narrative – it'll make your story more realistic if you're taking things from your own life, and you'll probably find those scenes easier to write. Of course, add a bit of drama and suspense to some of them if needed, and at other times just take something you've done in the past and use it as a starting point for an idea. There are lots of ways you can write what you know.

- Make use of history, and especially local history, in your writing; add an element of real life to your work and honour your local area at the same time. Head down to your nearest library and spend some time researching your town or county. Make use of the files and newspapers they have there, and really start to get a sense of what happened in the past where you live. It can be fun to do – like investigating – and it can add a nice touch to your work.

- Try writing some fanfic to get into the creative zone. Some people often find this easier than starting a whole new project from scratch, as if they already love a TV show or film, they'll already know the characters and locations like the back of their hand. Choose a favourite programme and start writing a story involving that world. If you end up writing more and finishing it, put it up on a fanfic website/forum and get some feedback – inspiration + writing help = a good deal.

- Write blogs, no matter what you end up blogging about. This can get you into the routine of writing every day (or every week), and it'll help show your potential readers what you're all about. Blog about writing or refer to your writing in your blogs for some cross-promotion, and you can even make money by recommending products or by taking part in affiliation schemes. You can read some of my own blog posts in the Blog Examples section of the appendix.

- Try typing nonsense. You spend so long thinking and planning that sometimes all you feel like doing is typing rubbish until something wonderful comes out – just think of all those monkeys and the complete works of Shakespeare (not that I'm comparing you to a monkey). Type nonsense words simply to get you into the action of typing, and soon you could be typing sentences that actually make sense (which is always good when you're a writer). It's all about getting around that block in your brain. You can physically type stuff into a word processor, so what's stopping you from writing that book? Nothing!

- Make use of a ghostwriter (for a bit). This doesn't mean getting someone to ghostwrite your whole book for you (although some writers do actually do this), but you can use a ghostwriter (or friend, or a writer you know online) to get back into the zone. Have them write a paragraph or two for the start of the book, or ask them for help with a scene that's caused you to get stuck. You can always rewrite it yourself afterwards, but if you leave any of the other person's words in, it's best to acknowledge them for their help and give them credit.

- As well as writing your novel, write any extras you'll need to use once it's finished – your book blurb, your author bio, and any marketing or sales copy. This will help get you prepared, and it will help you to tell your brain that you're serious about getting your book released. Come up with a release date and send out press releases to give yourself a self-imposed deadline that you can't ignore!

- If you're really having trouble writing anything, start by using some writing prompts to get you thinking. You don't have to use the stories you write from them, but it might be enough to get you back writing your own novel. I've created some of my own prompts for you in the Writing Prompts section of the appendix.

- Join a local book club to get you reading more widely and to get socialising. If there aren't any, suggest creating a book club with your friends – you can alternate who hosts each month, and you can make it more of an occasion by providing wine and nibbles.

- Look up literary festivals and writing workshops near you, and attend them to learn, network, and feel part of a literary community. You might even get to hear your favourite author speak, and anything that gets a lone writer out and socialising is a good thing.

- Find a writer who you can look up to and ask for advice, especially if they write in the same genre as you – having a mentor can sometimes make all the difference.
- Learn when to let your draft go out into the world, no matter how hard it is. The appropriate time to do this will be different for each writer, but let the thought of other people reading your draft motivate you to get it finished.
- Learn to ignore bad reviews. Either take something from them and use it when writing your next book, or ignore them. Don't raise to the bait, and remember that some readers get suspicious of consistently highly-rated books and might even prefer to see a few one or two star reviews to know there are 'real' readers interested in your work.
- Even if you only write as a hobby, think of all the potential careers you can have as a writer and let them inspire you to go out and write as much as you can. You might want to think outside the box on this one – you never know where you might end up.

There are more ideas in the main text of these books, but I hope this list has given you some motivation and inspiration to get writing. Go on, get writing now!

Writing Prompts

Writing prompts are a great way of getting you to (yep, you've guessed it) write. It doesn't matter if you never use these words, or if they're the biggest load of rubbish you've ever typed, just as long as it gets you into that creative writing headspace. Because of this, some of the following prompts are weird, wonderful, and just plain silly. Most work well if you're writing short stories or flash fiction, and who knows? You might get an idea for a novel from some of the words you come up with. Have fun!

The Beginnings Of A Story

Take these first sentences and turn them into a short story, whether it's a fun tale or a sinister scenario:

- The night was cold, and the pitter-patter of raindrops on the window was the only sound to be heard.

- This was it. This was Jimmy's big moment – this was his chance to show the world what he could do.

- 'Why did it always have to rain on Judgement Day?' thought Mark bitterly, as he looked up at the stormy sky.

- "Don't shoot!" shouted the policeman, holding his hands in the air.

- The walls of this room would always be grey; no matter what happened in the future, the past would always be here, soaked into the old bricks.

- When he woke from his dream, he was surprised to find that reality was far stranger than any of his nightmares could ever be.

- The balloon floated upwards into the cool night air, and she watched as it disappeared into the heavens.

- His teacher had always told him he'd never make anything of himself, that he'd never achieve anything in life. Well, he was going to show him.

- The cat jumped on her lap, purred, and settled down to sleep. She sighed as she stroked his soft fur; running the country would just have to wait.

- The keys on the keyboard were being pressed at lightning speed, the words of the novel pouring onto the page. The only problem was – they were doing it on their own.

- The dog was barking at something in the trees, and as the man walked over to the drooping branches, he saw what was driving his collie crazy…

- When you haven't had a mirror for over ten years, seeing your reflection can come as something of a shock.

- All at once, the birds stopped tweeting, the dog stopped barking, and the comforting chatter of the television switched off. It was coming.

- When he opened his door that morning, the snow was so high he couldn't even see the sky. Shivering, he made his way into the cold – he couldn't be late for this meeting, no matter what happened.

- The empty box seemed to be staring at her from across the room, as if it were judging her, as if it were reading her very thoughts.

- The rabbit hopped across the road in front of him, causing him to swerve madly to the left. As he careered over the cliff, his life flashed in front of his eyes. It was so boring he had to laugh.

- The woman staring out of the photo seemed to be looking right at him, looking through his very soul. He had to find out who she was, and he had to do it today.

- Roger threw the crumpled newspaper across the room. They always got it wrong, of course, but this time… this time they'd gone too far.

- As he waved his flag patriotically in the crowd, shouts reached his ears from across the courtyard. No, not shouts – screams.
- The house was falling apart around her and there was nothing she could do. Sitting down on the only chair left, she began to cry.

Questions To Answer In A Story

Come up with as weird an answer to one of these questions as you can, then see if any ideas come to you for a short story to write around it:

- What would happen if all technology broke for a month?
- What would happen if it stopped raining everywhere?
- What would happen if you woke up and your family had no idea who you were?
- What would happen if there was a chocolate shortage in the entire country?
- What would happen if the government folded in every single country?
- What would happen if you found out there was one person ruling the entire world?
- What would happen if animals suddenly started speaking English?
- What would happen if the dead started coming

back to life (non-zombies)?

- What would happen if you found your way to an alternate dimension?
- What would happen if you started being able to hear everyone's thoughts?
- What would happen if an earthquake hit your town and devastated the whole area?
- What would happen if plants suddenly came to life?
- What would happen if you switched bodies with someone for a day?
- What would happen if your place of work received a bomb threat?
- What would happen if you suddenly forgot your entire childhood?
- What would happen if you developed a hundred phobias in a day?
- What would happen if you got addicted to dancing?
- What would happen if you found you couldn't physically look away from your computer screen?
- What would happen if you suddenly realised what the meaning of life was?
- What would happen if you started craving the most bizarre foods in the world?

Themes/Ideas To Explore In A Story

Take one of these themes (or more) and try and come up with a story to base around it.

- When power goes to a person's head.
- Do we rely too much on technology?
- What if love isn't enough?
- Fighting for freedom.
- Coming of age/the difficulties of growing up.
- Becoming isolated, both physically and psychologically.
- Injustice/Truth vs. Justice.
- Fear of death and how to conquer it.
- Going into survival mode.
- Manipulation and control.
- When jealousy takes hold of someone.
- Good vs. Evil, in all its forms.
- Chasing your dreams.
- Identity – what it means and how to find yours.
- The breakdown of a relationship.
- The lengths someone would go to in order to protect their family.
- Doing the wrong things for good reasons.
- Getting revenge.
- Insanity – how do we know when we're going insane?
- Nature vs. Nurture.

The Alphabet Of Short Stories

You may think that you're completely out of ideas, even for short stories and small writing exercises to get you in the creative zone. When I think this, I do a little thing involving the alphabet: I come up with a word or phrase for each letter, and once I've gone from A-Z, I look down the list and see if there's anything that stands out to me. Then I write about that thing, whatever it may be (and sometimes, it's pretty weird). Here's an alphabet example to get you started:

A. Aliens
B. Broken doll
C. Car won't start
D. Dead quiet
E. Evil family member
F. Ferry
G. Grocers at night
H. Hospital is empty
I. Internet goes wrong
J. Jewel with powers
K. Killer kitchen
L. Loser gets even
M. Monopoly game goes wrong
N. No one can hear you
O. Overgrown maze in a park
P. Possessed toy
Q. Queen bee

R. Rogue snake

S. Strange smells

T. Traffic problem

U. Umbrella shortage

V. Vines going crazy

W. Wine overload

X. X-ray shows something unexpected

Y. Year of danger

Z. Zimmer frame malfunction

Character Prompts

Creating characters – especially secondary characters who may not be in your story/novel much – can be difficult for some people. How do you make them different enough to everyone else? How do you make them interesting when they're not around for that long? If they're going to pop up again later, how do you ensure your readers will remember who they are? It's certainly tricky, but spending some time with some character prompts can help. Just take one or two of the following and build up a character around the details given. More of this can be seen in the 'World Building Cheat Sheets' section of the appendix, but here are some ideas to get you started for now:

- Kieran Flanagan. A middle-aged Irish pub owner who's arrived in London to open up his own Irish bar. Tall, slim, and with dark curly hair, he's a hit with all the ladies.

- Dorothy Turner. A seventy-year-old retired nurse, she still helps out in her local community when she can, and she often visits her older neighbours who can't get out much anymore.

- Lisa Hatwell. A young, pretty blonde woman who knows how to use her looks to get what she wants. She's ruthless, cunning, but has a heart underneath her ice cold facade - it can just be pretty hard to find it.

- Johnny Willis. A fifty-year-old ex-con who's been toughened up by life in prison. Very mysterious and quiet, no one knows what he was in for.

- Jeremy Higgins. A friendly yet slightly bizarre thirty-something who seems to pop up all over the town. He lives on his own with his dog, and never seems to work or do anything to earn money. No one knows much about him, despite his constant presence.

Writing Quotes

Here are some of my favourite quotes to do with writing, success, and motivation, scoured from the internet:

"There is nothing to writing. All you do is sit down at a typewriter and bleed." (Ernest Hemingway)

"If there's a book that you want to read, but it hasn't been written yet, then you must write it." (Toni Morrison)

"If you don't have time to read, you don't have the time (or the tools) to write. Simple as that." (Stephen King)

"We write to taste life twice, in the moment and in retrospect." (Anaïs Nin)

"Fantasy is hardly an escape from reality. It's a way of understanding it." (Lloyd Alexander)

"And by the way, everything in life is writable about if you have the outgoing guts to do it, and the imagination to improvise. The worst enemy to creativity is self-doubt." (Sylvia Plath, *The Unabridged Journals of Sylvia Plath*)

"No tears in the writer, no tears in the reader. No surprise in the writer, no surprise in the reader." (Robert Frost)

"You must stay drunk on writing so reality cannot destroy you." (Ray Bradbury, *Zen in the Art of Writing*)

"Fiction is the truth inside the lie." (Stephen King)

"Don't tell me the moon is shining; show me the glint of light on broken glass." (Anton Chekhov)

"After nourishment, shelter and companionship, stories are the thing we need most in the world." (Philip Pullman)

"How vain it is to sit down to write when you have not stood up to live." (Henry David Thoreau)

"The scariest moment is always just before you start." (Stephen King, *On Writing: A Memoir of the Craft*)

"Either write something worth reading or do something worth writing." (Benjamin Franklin)

"Writing means sharing. It's part of the human condition to want to share things – thoughts, ideas, opinions." (Paulo Coelho)

"Writing is an exploration. You start from nothing and learn as you go." (E.L. Doctorow)

"Good writing is supposed to evoke sensation in the reader – not the fact that it is raining, but the feeling of being rained upon." (E.L. Doctorow)

"Writing a book of poetry is like dropping a rose petal down the Grand Canyon and waiting for the echo." (Don Marquis)

"While writing, I tend to repeat the same song, endlessly, for thousands of times. This helps me ignore any lyrics, and helps create a consistent mood for each book." (Chuck Palahniuk)

"Prose is architecture, not interior decoration." (Ernest Hemingway)

"To produce a mighty book, you must choose a mighty theme." (Herman Melville)

"It is perfectly okay to write garbage – as long as you edit brilliantly." (C.J. Cherryh)

"First, find out what your hero wants, then just follow him!" (Ray Bradbury)

"I love deadlines. I like the whooshing sound they make as they fly by." (Douglas Adams)

Thanks to the following websites for these quotes: Goodreads, Brainyquote.com and Writer's Digest.

Other Inspirational Quotes

"Put your heart, mind, and soul into even your smallest acts. This is the secret of success." (Swami Sivananda)

"Nothing is impossible, the word itself says 'I'm possible'!" (Audrey Hepburn)

"If opportunity doesn't knock, build a door." (Milton Berle)

"Change your thoughts and you can change your world." (Norman Vincent Peale).

"Believe you can and you're halfway there." (Theodore Roosevelt)

"Follow your bliss and the universe will open doors where there were only walls." (Joseph Campbell)

"Nurture your mind with great thoughts. To believe in the heroic makes heroes." (Benjamin Disraeli)

"Luck is a dividend of sweat. The more you sweat, the luckier you get." (Ray Kroc)

"Either you run the day, or the day runs you." (Jim Rohn)

"Do not go where the path may lead, go instead where there is no path and leave a trail." (Ralph Waldo Emerson)

"The journey of a thousand miles begins with one step." (Lao Tzu)

"We are what we repeatedly do. Excellence, therefore, is not an act but a habit." (Aristotle)

"Dream big and dare to fail." (Norman Vaughan)

"With will one can do anything." (Samuel Smiles)

"Do not wait to strike till the iron is hot; but make it hot by striking." (William B. Sprague)

"Nothing will ever be attempted if all possible objections must first be overcome." (Samuel Johnson)

"Believe with all of your heart that you will do what you were made to do." (Orison Swett Marden)

Thanks to the following websites for these quotes: Brainyquote.com, Keepinspiring.me and Inspirational-Quotes.info.

Creative Playlists

Music is incredibly useful when it comes to being creative and getting writing. You can use it to help you concentrate (especially if there are other noises in and outside your house that you want to drown out), you can use it to motivate yourself to get something done, and you can use it to soothe and relax you when you need a break from that screen.

Here are a few short playlists you can use (and add to) when writing or starting to write. All of these playlists were found using Spotify, and it's incredibly easy to create your own playlist for your thinking, writing and relaxing sessions. You can also find similar things on YouTube and other sites/music apps. Some of these tracks are a little cheesy, but what's life without a bit of cheese now and again?

Relaxation Playlists – Give your brain a rest!

Barefoot Bliss Out by Spotify UK
Slow Down by Spotify UK
Chill Hits by Spotify
Totally Stress Free by Spotify
Mellow Beats by Spotify
Hanging Out and Relaxing by Spotify
Stress Relief by Spotify
Lost In The Clouds by Spotify
Mellow Morning by Spotify
Sweet Soul Chillout by Spotify Sverige

Motivational Playlists – You can do this!

Endorphin Rush by Spotify
Themes From the Movies by Spotify
Motivational Songs by Carlos Piles Zaro
Motivation for work by Lindomar Jon-Ming
100 Most Motivational Songs by Topsify
Rise & Shine Motivation by SpinGrey
Rock Motivation by yourlifepalestra
Songs for Success by Acn On Rotation
Power Hits by Digster Italy
Feeling Motivated by Ian Wu

Concentration Playlists – Write away!

Deep Focus by Spotify
Music for Concentration by Spotify UK
Acoustic Concentration by Spotify

Brain Food by Spotify
Productive Morning by Spotify
Instrumental Study by Spotify
Indie Folk for Focus by Spotify
Nice & Easy Workflow by Spotify
Relax & Focus by Spotify
ThinkTank by Spotify

Travel Playlists – To accompany your literary tour or just for getting away from that screen!

Ultimate Road Trip by Spotify UK
Alt. Rock Roadtrip by Spotify UK
Driving Songs by Topsify UK
Classic Road Trip Songs by Spotify
Long Way Home by Spotify
Globe Trotting by Spotify
Alternative Route by Spotify
Highway 61 by Spotify
Music For An Unfamiliar Road by Spotify UK
The Southern Highway Chronicles by Spotify Norway

World Building Cheat Sheets

World building for your novel or series of novels can be a long and complicated task, but it can also be really fun. How often do you get to create entire worlds? You can choose what your city or town or village is like, you can choose who lives where, where your main characters hang out, and a million other little details that will really make your book come to life. For sci-fi and fantasy genres, you can pretty much do whatever you want in the world you're creating, turning everything upside down if you wish to. What I'm going to focus on in this section is simpler – this is for if your story is based mainly in the 'real' world, but you need to create believable people and places to populate your novel with.

Here are just a few ideas and questions to get you thinking about your own world, from the locations to the characters and other bits and bobs it can be worth planning before you start writing your novel.

Locations

Here are some location questions to get you thinking.

Let's start with the simple stuff:

What is the name of your location?
What is the type of setting (village/town/city/other)?
What country is it set in?
Whereabouts (roughly) in the country is the location supposed to be? E.g. Is it landlocked or by the coast?
What is the rough population?
Are all of your locations fictional or will you be using/referring to real places too?
Where does your main character live?
Where do your secondary characters live in relation to your main character?
How would you describe the place in basic terms – rural/urban? Posh/rough? Desirable/cheap to live in?
How would you describe the location if it were on a postcard?
What is the terrain like?
Are there any tourist attractions, and if so, what are they?
Are there any pubs/bars/clubs, and if so, what are they?
Are there any restaurants, and if so, what are they?
Are there any town hall type places? Any councils or government buildings?
Are there any libraries/theatres?
Are there any historical sites – castles, stately homes, or similar places of interest?
Are there police stations/fire stations/hospitals/doctors?
What kinds of shops and services are available there?
Is there a prison?
What fun things are there to do there?
Is there any countryside/are there places to walk around the area?
Are there lakes, rivers, or other bodies of water?

OK, now let's get down to the nitty gritty (this will depend heavily on your chosen genre, but as an example, I'm thinking of crime/murder mystery type books):

Are there any dark secrets in your location's past?
Have there been any murders in the area? If so, what are the details and when did they occur?
Who runs the location? Local council, local members of parliament, mayor, police?
Who runs it unofficially? Is there a rich businessman who oversees the place? Are there any illegal gangs or people with dodgy connections pulling the strings?
Describe your character's house – the number of rooms, the layout, the exterior, the garden. Is it a council house? Is it an old building? Is it an expensive new build with all the best quality furnishings? What does it say about your character (and their family, if necessary)?
Are the other houses in the area similar or do they differ? Describe a few different houses.
Describe the main population in terms of age, social class, race, and so on.
Describe the location in great detail (and/or draw a map). Include road names, locations of houses and businesses, pathways that your main character usually takes, where they work, and other places of interest. Make sure they all work together for the purposes of your plot, and if you're planning a series, think ahead to what else you need to include in the area.

If you're writing sci-fi or fantasy, the questions you need to ask yourself will obviously be different to these, and they'll probably go deeper into the hierarchy of your characters, how the place is run and by whom, and the general government/ruling party and how things work on a daily basis. If you're setting your novel in the normal world, it will be more basic, but don't make the mistake of keeping it *too* basic; your readers need to feel that this place – this world – exists, and the settings you use are just as important as your characters and your story.

Characters

Creating characters for your novel can be fun, but it can be harder than you think, especially once you've got past your protagonist, your antagonist, and your other main characters. As you get into the minor characters, how do you make sure they're different enough from each other? How can you make sure your readers won't get confused? How can you make sure that you, the writer, won't get confused?

It's a simple thing, but I find that creating a thorough character profile for each person – no matter how minor or how little they are involved in the plot – can really help. You can do this in a variety of ways, from typing it into Word, writing it in a notepad so you can have easy access to it when you're writing, or even using computer programs that give you space to write down character information (think Scrivener, for example). Some people also find it useful to add images to their character profiles, whether from drawings they've done themselves, people they've found on Google Images, or photos they've found on one of the stock photos site. You can even use images of celebrities for guidance, but this doesn't always work for everyone – once you've pictured Johnny Depp or Matt Damon in your lead role, you'll find it hard to picture anyone else.

So, what to put in the actual character profile? You can add in any amount of detail that you want, but I've come up with a few questions for you to answer so you can really get a feel for your character, and so you can understand their actions and motivations. It's not just about what they look like, or what job they do, or who they live with – you've really got to get to the bottom of the characters' pasts, feelings, and personalities. You've got to think of them as real people, because to your readers, they will be (well, hopefully, anyway!)

Here are some character profile questions to get you thinking. Let's start with the simple stuff:

Name?
DOB?
Relationship status?
Physical appearance?
Any scars or tattoos?
Style – what kind of clothes do they like wearing?
What is their job?
What qualifications do they have?
Where is their place of residence?
Who do they live with?
Who is in their close and extended family?
Who are their main friends?
Where did they go to school?
Main likes?
Main dislikes?
Do they own any pets?
Favourite band, TV show and film?

OK, now let's get down to the nitty gritty:

Have they ever been in love? If so, describe their partner and how they fell for each other.

What is their biggest regret in life?

What are their biggest fears?

What activities and places to visit are on their bucket list?

How would they react if they found themselves in a fight?

What would they say are their best features / personality traits?

What would they say are their worst features / personality traits?

What three celebrities – dead or alive – would they have at their fantasy dinner party?

What is their most secret desire?

What is their dream occupation?

Name something they've never told anyone about:

What is their most embarrassing moment?

What qualities do they most admire in the opposite sex?

What qualities do they look for in their friends?

How do they relate to their family members?

Describe a past event that had a big impact on their life:

What is their favourite quote (funny, inspirational, motivational etc)?

Who do they most admire in the whole world and why?

What is the worst thing they've ever done in their life?

What is the craziest thing they've ever done in their life?

What are their goals and ambitions?

Well, you get the idea. You need to get inside your characters' heads, and make sure you know everything about them. Of course, you don't need to go into quite as much detail for the really minor characters, but just thinking about this will help you when you need to write a difficult scene, or when you don't know how they'd react under certain circumstances, or if you're not sure what they'd say when confronted by someone they didn't like. Just look at what you've written down about their personality and their past, and apply that to the scene. The more you do this, the easier it will become.

So, why not try filling in a character profile for your protagonist right now? It will help you with your book, and more than anything else, it can be a pretty fun task to do! Your characters will thank you for it.

Literary Tourism Travel Plan

Travelling is a great way of resetting your mind, getting inspiration for stories, and giving yourself that well-deserved break. But for writers, there's an alternative to the usual road trips and sunning yourself by the pool – why not try some literary tourism? I've been to a few places on this list, but I'd love to visit more. This type of travelling should be both eye-opening and inspiring for any budding (or established) writer, so if you get the chance, why not look up some of these tourist attractions?

I've listed some of the more popular ones here, split up into countries/territories for ease if you're thinking about making your own literary travelling itinerary, and you can find out all about each place online. This is just to get you thinking about the opportunities of literary tourism – perhaps for your next trip? Get inspired by visiting the places these famous writers lived, worked, and died.

United Kingdom & Ireland

- Charles Dickens Museum / House, London
- Oscar Wilde's Childhood Home, Dublin
- Bronte Parsonage Museum, West Yorkshire
- Monk's House, East Sussex (Virginia and Leonard Woolf home, hub for Bloomsbury Group activity)
- Jane Austen's House & Museum, Hampshire, England
- Stokesay Court, Shropshire (where the film version of *Atonement* was filmed)
- Thomas Hardy's Cottage, Dorset
- Hill Top, Cumbria (Beatrix Potter's farmhouse)
- Shaw's Corner, Hertfordshire (George Bernard Shaw's country home)
- King's Cross Train Station, Platform 9 3/4 (*Harry Potter*)
- Shakespeare's Globe Theatre, London
- Shakespeare's Birthplace, Stratford-upon-Avon, Warwickshire
- The British Library, London
- Sherlock Holmes Museum, London
- Keats House (John Keats), Hampstead, London
- Poets' Corner, Westminster Abbey
- The Old Curiosity Shop, London (Charles Dickens)
- Dr Johnson's House, London

United States & Canada

- Mark Twain House & Museum, Connecticut
- Mark Twin Birthplace / Boyhood Home and Museum, Missouri
- Ernest Hemingway Birthplace, Illinois
- Edgar Allan Poe's grave, Baltimore, Maryland
- Herman Melville's grave, Woodlawn Cemetery, The Bronx, New York
- Emily Dickinson Museum, Massachusetts
- The Mount (Edith Wharton's Home), Massachusetts
- Kurt Vonnegut Memorial Library, Indianapolis, Indiana
- Truman Capote's Apartment, Brooklyn, New York
- HP Lovecraft sites, Providence, Rhode Island
- Walden Pond, Concord, Massachusetts (influenced Henry David Thoreau)
- City Lights Books, San Francisco, California
- Edgar Allan Poe Museum, Richmond, Virginia
- F Scott Fitzgerald's Birthplace, St Paul, Minnesota
- John Updike's Home, Shillington, Pennsylvania
- Green Gables, Cavendish, Canada
- Henry Miller Memorial Library, Big Sur, California

- Sleepy Hollow Cemetery, Sleepy Hollow, New York

Other

- Nietzsche-Haus, Sils-Maria, Switzerland
- Karl Marx House, Trier, Germany
- Franz Kafka's grave, The New Jewish Cemetery, Prague

Get travelling and get inspired!

Your Writing Wall

Throughout my books you've probably noticed that I advise covering the wall by your writing desk with all kinds of weird and wonderful things to help inspire you or motivate you. This may not appeal to everyone, especially if you like to keep your writing area neat and tidy, but even just one thing (framed nicely if you wish) hung on the wall can really help when you find yourself with a bit of a creative block.

As I mentioned, I have a page from a newspaper on the wall behind my writing desk at home, reminding me how far I've come and that someone was interested enough in me to ask to interview me for my local paper. It doesn't matter if it makes you look a bit cheesy, as most likely not many people are going to see it anyway, and also, it's just for you. It's one in a long line of little things you can do to keep yourself motivated every day (or whenever you have time to write).

Here's a list of possible things you can put on your own wall to help you with motivating yourself:

- A premade cover that you've had designed for

the very purpose of self-motivation.

- If you haven't gone that far with the cover, at least some pictures and the title of your book in a suitable font so you can picture what your final book will look like.
- 3D mockups of your book cover to really picture what it'll look like.
- Any local newspaper or magazine articles on you or your writing (or on another local author whom you respect and admire).
- Anything you've created yourself in terms of marketing your author self – business cards, flyers, adverts.
- Drawings you've done of your own characters/setttings/scenes.
- Images found online of people resembling your characters/the locations in your story.
- A picture of the cover of your favourite book.
- A picture of your favourite author or favourite character.
- Infographics about writing - statistics and so on regarding self-publishing or information regarding book sales of your favourite authors.
- If you've already written the opening to your book (or a killer scene later on that you started with), print that out and stick it on your wall. Remind yourself that you can write (because, look! You wrote that), and that you can continue writing the rest of your book. You just need to keep typing.
- If you've already got books out there and have been receiving reviews, why not put a few of them onto a page and stick it on your wall? Bonus points if the reviews are from people you

don't know rather than friends and family (although any reviews are nice if they're good ones).

- Inspirational quotes from famous people, and also ones you've just heard and liked.
- Any encouraging emails from friends/family/fans about your writing.
- A picture representing why you're doing this. It may be fame and/or fortune, nothing wrong with that, or it may be because you're dedicating the book to someone (in which case, put a photo of them on the wall to help you get motivated), or to prove to someone you can do it (again, the same thing, unless it's someone you really don't want staring down at you while you work).
- Literary Posters. You can get great posters these days, featuring artwork from novels and even entire novels written out to form a picture. Personally, I have a map of the UK on the wall in my writing office which is made up with the names of hundreds of English, Scottish, Welsh and Irish writers.
- Some quotes written by yourself to give yourself that much-needed kick up the arse! They can be as simple as 'You can do this!' to something a bit more convoluted to think about, like 'Time will pass, and soon another year will be gone. If you write every day, you could have a book done by the end of this year. If you don't, you'll have spent another year wishing you could be a writer. Stop wishing and write now!'

Basically, put something on your wall that will motivate you every time you experience a bit of a writing slump

– it works for me, and it could work for you too.

Blog Examples

As I mentioned in the main text, blogs are a great way of teaching yourself how to sit down and write (every day, every week, or every month), no matter what subject you decide to blog about: writing, reading, food, travel, animals… as long as you're writing, it's good practice, and it can help to build your online platform.

If you want your blog readers to know that you're a writer, the best way to do this is either blog about writing, or blog about themes and subjects that you can relate back to your writing. This can be done directly or indirectly, but it's always worth adding a link to your books at the end (or down the side of the main text), so that if people enjoyed what you wrote, they can check out more of your writing.

Here is an example of a blog post I wrote on a subject that I could link back to my own writing (this was written a couple of years ago). It also happens to be a subject that I'm interested in anyway, which always helps!

Medium Rare: Magic and Mysticism in Fiction and Life

My 'Little Forest' series of novels ('The Former World', 'Memento Mori' and 'The Exalted') focus on aspects of the paranormal which, for most people, are only found in the realm of fiction: communicating with the dead, clairvoyance, telepathy, extrasensory perception, and other magical and mystical powers that seemingly only belong in the pages of a horror or fantasy book.

I, like many other authors, take inspiration from popular culture, modern society and contemporary artists, but even though 'The Former World' and the other books in my series are set in modern-day England, I had to take a long, dark journey into the past to start my research. A metaphorical journey, of course; while I may be open to ideas of the supernatural, I don't claim to be able to travel back in time. Yet…

Hundreds of years ago, it was quite normal to be walking down the street in your village and to overhear gossip about the local cunning-man or cunning-woman: people who claimed to be able to find your lost or stolen property, identify criminals, or cure you of an ailment, all by magical means. At least, I'm guessing it was normal – as I said, I don't *actually* have a time machine (yet).

My point is, people in the sixteenth, seventeenth, eighteenth, even nineteenth centuries believed in normal-looking people who had extraordinary powers. They believed in curses, spells, divination, magic, and necromancy. It was a mystical world, where the forests were home to hermits calling themselves wizards, where the country seemed much bigger and the medical options much smaller, where magic was something that was not only believed in, but was extremely common.

Fast forward to the twenty-first century. We still have wizards (although mainly in the form of Harry Potter and other fictional magical men), and we still have most of everything else, albeit in a much more diluted way, but there's one key thing that's missing (at least, for the majority of people): belief.

Now, I'm aware that some people believe in all of these paranormal subjects as much as our ancestors did hundreds of years ago, and I realise why, for others, that belief has faded – all of the advancements in science, the growing infrastructure and international media, instant access to information, logical explanations being provided for strange phenomena – but the mystery of it still intrigues me.

In my most recent novel in the Little Forest series, 'The Exalted', we meet a rather suspicious character, 'Marvin the Mystic' (real name, Terence). He claims to be able to speak to the dead, and embarks on a career of being a medium, ranging from private readings to dramatic theatre shows. This, of course, annoys the main character, Beth Powers, who knows for certain that he can't see the spirits he claims to be able to see. She doesn't like the fact that he's making money from (and taking the piss out of) vulnerable people – people who wish to hear from their dead loved ones – and that's the problem, really, isn't it?

We don't believe in magic and the supernatural because we don't want to be taken for a ride, we don't want to be taken advantage of, we don't want to be made fun of or be made a fool of. In this day and age, this is understandable: you can barely do anything or go anywhere without people knowing about it. So-called friends tag you in places and photos on Facebook, they tweet what you're doing to an audience of thousands, they record you on their phone and upload it to Youtube to an audience of millions. A few hundred years ago, if you wanted to visit a cunning-man for help, you just wandered over to his hovel under cover of darkness, without having to worry about getting caught on CCTV or being pranked by some hidden-camera show.

I remember a television programme a few years ago made by the lovely Derren Brown: 'Derren Brown Investigates: The Man Who Contacts The Dead'. Now, I'll try not to gush too much, but I'm a massive fan of Derren. I've seen every single TV show he's ever done, and I've attended all but one of his amazing stage shows. If you haven't heard of him, you need to look him up: he's charming, he's funny, he's clever, and he has a deliciously dark streak... dastardly, you might say – just watch the recent 'Apocalypse' two-part special and you'll see what I mean. But his stunts, his tricks, his explorations and exposés always have a point to them, and of course, the point of 'The Man Who Contacts The Dead' was to highlight the fact that many mediums aren't what they claim to be. There has been, inevitably, a lot of controversy over this (as with most of Derren's shows – for example, he recently convinced a life-long atheist scientist of God's presence in just 15 minutes), and it just goes to show that even in the twenty-first century, there are people willing to stand up for both sides.

When I think about it, Derren has covered pretty much all of the themes and subjects which are explored in my Little Forest series (and in my own short stories – some of which have been released as a collection under the title 'Grown By The Wicked Moon'): talking to the dead, spiritualism, religion, zombie outbreaks (that's right, you heard me), psychology, manipulation, and the power one person can hold over another. Derren has made perfectly normal citizens stage an armed robbery, he's convinced someone he's committed a murder, and manipulated a man into 'shooting' English national treasure, Stephen Fry. He's turned someone into a miraculous faith-healer, predicted the lottery numbers, staged a terrifying (and fake) séance, and played Russian Roulette live on television. He also made an entire town believe in a lucky dog statue, the devilish rogue (note: this wasn't the sole point of that particular show). It's quite a CV. I think his 'Investigates' show did a lot to change opinions on mediums, or at least it got people thinking about the subject who may not have come across it in their daily lives before. It warned the public of the possible crooks and frauds out there, and while I'm by no means against all mediums, the show was good for exposing how they went about their work.

My own personal views on spiritualism aside (which, if you're interested, is a lot of cynicism mixed with cautious optimism at the idea that bona fide mediums could exist, or at least have done in the past), I wanted to end with a suggestion.

The worlds of the paranormal, the supernatural, the afterlife, the mystical realms and the magical people, is all fascinating. It's a bit morbid, a bit sinister, and very intriguing. We love the idea of it, we love discussing it, we love questioning it and debating it until the wee hours when surrounded by friends and large quantities of alcohol. It is one of the ultimate questions: what happens to us when we die?

Mediums and fortune-tellers can be a bit of fun, and whether they're legit or not, they make for good entertainment. Like many people, I get uncomfortable when they start delivering specific messages from the dead, especially if those messages make the intended recipient burst into tears, but generally they fire up the imagination and get you wondering: *could* it be true?

As long as humans live, I think there will always be questions asked about the meaning of life, ponderings concerning what happens when we die, wonderments regarding the possibility of talking to the dead. And personally, I hope that people never stop asking these questions, no matter what science may tell us in the future, and no matter how sceptical we become as a society. Because as long as we keep the prospect alive, we're somehow linking back to our ancestors, the ones who swept through the forest in long, black cloaks, hunting out the local wise men and muttering enchantments under their breath to keep away the evil. (I don't know about you, but if I lived in those times, I'd definitely make sure I wore a long, black coat. Preferably one that swooshed round corners dramatically – I'll get one ready for when someone invents time travel).

It is much like when I'm watching a magic show (the theatrical, rabbit-out-of-a-hat, lady-cut-in-half-while-wearing-not-many-clothes type of magic show): although part of me wants to know how the tricks are done, part of me *really* doesn't. I like the mystery, I like the intrigue, I like the not knowing.

Some mediums and fortune tellers may well be fake, and as long as they're not hurting anyone, I'm OK with that.They're one of the last links to our mystical past, one of the last connections to the weird and wonderful world of spiritualism, one of the last reminders of just how strange the universe – and us humans – can be. I suggest that while we should keep our eyes open for people who may rip us off, we should also embrace the strangeness, embrace the past, and embrace the magic.

I don't know about you, but give me a bit of mystery any day.

***

Here's another blog post I wrote (again about a subject I'm interested in) in order to promote my first book, *The Former World*, the climax of which is set at Hallowe'en. I added in some personal things about me and how I remember my Hallowe'ens as a kid in order to inject some sense of self into the blog:

Taking Back Hallowe'en

It's coming up to that time of year again, when the leaves start falling from the trees, the nights start drawing in, and everyone starts longing for the lightness and delicate beauty of summer. The weather turns bleak, the wind blows shrilly through the night, and before you know it, ghouls and ghosts start creeping out of the shadows and into your towns, your villages, your houses. I believe October is the best month in the year, and if you've read any of my writing, especially my debut novel, you'll know why: Hallowe'en.

I know some people don't like Hallowe'en because its religious background is usually completely ignored and replaced by gimmicks. The costumes, the makeup, the trick-or-treating... adults generally don't like the idea of having to dish out sweets in order to stop the neighbours' kids from egging their house. But that's not the only thing that Hallowe'en is about, and for all of you out there who usually hate this holiday, I urge you to reconsider.

Think back to your childhood and discover the nostalgic side of Hallowe'en: the memories that come flooding back when you smell a toffee apple, the emotions that filter through your (usually frozen) body when you see a stall selling sticky fudge or bags of sweets. The slight fizzle of fear that still runs up your spine when you see someone in a particularly authentic costume, perhaps one you remember from your youth as scaring the absolute crap out of you.

Call me weird, but I love it. I love the whole idea of Hallowe'en, the underlying message, the challenge it throws at you every year: come as you aren't. Dare to be different. Be who you really want to be, if only just for one night.

My love of Hallowe'en and all things spooky slowly crept up on me during my childhood, becoming more and more ingrained with every October 31st that went by. I live in a small village in Staffordshire, England, and on the edge of that village lies a stately home where my mum used to work when I was young. (If anyone's read my novel 'The Former World', you'll recognise much of Chillingsley Hall in the following description). In the daytime it is magnificent, elegant, and beautiful. Awe-inspiring, even, to a little girl. When it gets dark, however, it's a whole different story. When it gets dark, the ghosts come out to play.

I have an extremely vivid memory of walking through the amazing gardens, all sinister and menacing in the darkness, and tentatively entering the courtyard to see the mansion house lit up – its huge, white pillars twinkling under all the spotlights. The grounds had been transformed; there were food and drink stalls everywhere, filling the air with intermingling smells of barbecued meat, cinnamon-fused mulled wine and sugary delights. Endless throngs of ghosts, witches, vampires, and fairy tale characters milled around, filling the place with a vibrant, magical energy. The thought that many of these creatures lived in the same village as me had seemed completely unreal.

The main thing that stayed with me from that Hallowe'en was visiting 'Doctor Death' in the mansion house. As you can imagine, the sight of a mad doctor, covered in blood and flinging entrails at people (in a nice, festive kind of way) really affected me. When I looked a bit more closely and realised that underneath all the white makeup, grime, and fake blood, the doctor was actually my *mum*, it affected me somewhat further. Mid-entrail-fling, she dropped the Doctor Death persona, smiled at me with blood-stained lips, and asked if I was having a good time. This freaked me out more than any ghoul or ghost could ever have done, and I believe I ran away screaming to the nearest fudge stall. I'd been well and truly spooked, and I'd loved it.

I also love the whole idea of dressing up at Hallowe'en, of creating a character so different to your daily self, because it's a lot like writing fiction. When I create a character, or when I create a world (like the county of Covershire in the Little Forest series), I find it the easiest part of the whole writing process. What's better than constructing a village, a town, a house, a group of friends, a murderer, all from your limitless imagination? You have no boundaries, no obstacles, nothing to stop you from conjuring up whatever enchanting little nuggets of magic you want to and making them as deliciously appealing to your reader as they already are to you.

Because that's what it is, really, when you stop and think about it. Magic. Hallowe'en is enchanting because it explores 'the other' – but not in some distant, abstract way like a horror movie or a second-hand ghost story. With Hallowe'en, you get to be right in the thick of it. You get to be who you want to be, and for one night only, you can get away with delighting in the macabre. Hell, it's even expected.

Over the years, Hallowe'en seems to have been twisted and turned into something unrecognisable from what it meant when many of us were children. Now it's all about getting drunk, university house parties and who can wear the sluttiest costume. I say we take Hallowe'en back. I say we take it back to its scary, exciting, bloodcurdling roots. I say we embrace the darker times of our childhoods, revel in the spooky celebrations, and create a magical, fictional world for ourselves. Just for one night.

Together, we'll take Hallowe'en back, one scream at a time.

***

Of course, sometimes, you just want to blog about things that interest you. It doesn't have to relate to your writing in any way - just liking your style of writing can be enough for someone to look up the rest of your work. Here's an example of a blog I wrote about something I'm interested in, vaguely related to literature (but more like TV and films):

Vampires: To Bite Or Not To Bite?

It seems to me that vampires have changed over the years – which is exactly the thing they're not supposed to do, of course – and films, TV shows, and books are all looking for ways to make vampires into something 'new'. They all want to put a twist on it; change their nature somehow, or change the rules. Sunlight? Pah! Stakes? Whatever. Garlic? Yeah right... This is understandable, but is the answer really to make them *so* different? Are we losing sight of what made them such intriguing, powerful, seductive creatures in the first place? Or is their evolution needed to keep the interest in them alive?

These days, you generally don't get ugly vampires. Let's just get that out there now. And I know, beauty is subjective and what one person finds attractive can be totally different to what another person finds attractive, but – bumpy-headed vamps aside – none of the leading vampire men or women have been acne-covered, obese monsters with bad hair and a B.O. problem.

Lestat. Louis de Pointe du Lac. Angel. Spike. Damon. Stefan. Bill. Eric. Edward. They might not all be your exact cup of tea, but they'd never be described as ugly. Compare this with the early vampires – Dracula, Nosferatu – and we can see how much things have changed. When the Count is first introduced in Bram Stoker's novel, he is described as so: "Within, stood a tall old man, clean shaven save for a long white moustache, and clad in black from head to foot, without a single speck of colour about him anywhere" (Bram Stoker, 1987). Of course, he changes as the story continues, but as entrances go, it's not the most glamorous or seductive ever written. And you only need to look at how Nosferatu is portrayed in F.W. Murnau's 1922 film to see that vamps have definitely changed in both appearance and their ability to charm.

So, looks aside, let's look at the practicalities of being a vamp. Back in Dracula's day, it was hard to be a badass vampire. 24 hour spooking was out of the question; daylight was a big no-no. He also couldn't enter a person's home unless invited, so having good social skills in order to talk his way in was something of a must.

The whole daylight thing isn't a problem in a novel or story, and you can get around it quite easily in a film, but when it comes to a TV series, it can be downright annoying, especially if your main vamp character regularly interacts with humans and other daylight-loving demons. This led to the necessity of coming up with new ways of getting around the problem of the sun. In *Buffy The Vampire Slayer*, there was one episode where Spike found a ring that allowed him to walk in the daylight, and I believe this method was utilised in *The Vampire Diaries* too. Spike generally got around in the daytime by covering himself with a coat or blanket, and hoping he got to where he wanted to go without frying. Later on in the *Buffy* series, he just took to hanging outside in the shade, so obviously sunlight wasn't *too* much of a problem. Not all shows try and get around the daylight issue, though – in *True Blood*, they not only can't go out in the daylight, but they get 'the bleeds' if they stay up past sunrise. They sleep in coffins or cubby-holes built into their house, something which most modern day vamps would scowl at.

In *Twilight*, the vampires can go out into the sun, and they also don't need to sleep at all, covering all bases and meaning that the action can happen anytime. Of course, when they *do* venture out into the daylight, they sparkle. Like diamonds. Or – in the films – just like they're a bit sweaty. So place them in a part of America that's generally gloomy and overcast, and problem solved.

Even though the film wasn't exactly well received, I think it's worth bringing up the Josh Hartnett-starring *30 Days Of Night* here, as I really like the concept: in an Alaskan town that doesn't see *any* sunlight for an entire month, the last thing you want is for some evil vamps to appear on the scene. With no daylight, there's no escape. I like how this harks back to the origins of vampires but gives it an interesting twist, and there are no suave and seductive Dracula types here, just bloodthirsty monsters.

Not being able to enter a place unless invited crops up in a lot of recent vampire shows and films, although, again, they've managed to get round it: for example, in *Buffy*, vampires can enter the local high school to terrorise the students – and the teachers – because of the Latin welcome sign above the door. You know, the one that means 'enter all ye who seek knowledge'. Angelus sought knowledge, got into the school, and killed a teacher. So that worked out well.

Then we come to the idea of 'neutered' vamps. This happens a lot in TV shows and films because it comes to a point when people just don't want simply *evil* vampires; they want monsters who have at least a tiny bit of humanity in them, so they can identify with them. Buffy only fell in love with Angel because he had a soul – when he was in his 'Angelus' state, she didn't like the 'running around and killing everyone' part of him, surprisingly. Spike – as a vamp who loved maiming and murdering – couldn't become a regular character. Give him a chip in his head and make him incapable of harming people, and he suddenly joined the regular cast. He changed from guzzling fresh human blood to pig's blood, or whatever kind of blood he could get in a plastic packet. In *Twilight*, the Cullen family are 'vegetarians' – which in their world, means sucking the blood from animals rather than humans. So not *exactly* vegetarians, then. The world of *True Blood* is based around the invention of a synthetic blood substitute that could sustain the vampire population after they 'came out' to the world. They weren't just monsters skulking in the shadows; they were out and they were proud. This is quite possibly the most modern idea I think I've seen regarding vampires in popular culture today, and in my humble opinion, it's one of the best vampire shows out there.

Like with *True Blood*, some other films have tried to take a different twist on the whole vampire idea. For example, *Daybreakers* looks at the possibility of vampires actually dying out – because they've fed on all the humans. I really liked this idea (not the idea of the human race being farmed for vampires, of course, but the fact that this is probably what *would* happen if vamps were real). It isn't an idea that is generally explored in typical vampire films and shows, but it seems like the most likely outcome if vampires did exist.

So – for modern day audiences – it seems that the vamps do have to be neutered in some way, so that it's acceptable to fall in love with them, to be friends with them, even to stand with them against some other kind of evil. They need to be sympathetic characters, and you don't need me to tell you that cold-blooded killers generally *aren't*.

What do you think of the ways in which vampires have changed over the years – in literature, film, and TV? Do you think we're losing sight of what they were meant to be? Do you prefer the new-fangled vamps who sparkle and can walk in the sun? How about the 90s versions – all leather and dark colours, lurking around in the shadows and brooding all the time? Is it a matter of what is the scariest or what is the most attractive? Which vamps are the most interesting – the ones cowering in the darkness or the ones embracing the light? Good vamps or bad vamps – which do you prefer? While writing this article I kept thinking of one thing: what would Bram Stoker think of all the different types of vampires in popular culture today? Would he be impressed? Or would he be turning in his grave? (Assuming he hasn't already risen from it...) What do *you* think?

(Note: any mistakes in this blog post are completely mine – most of this was written from memory of the films and TV shows mentioned, and unlike the immortal vamps, my memory tends to fade with time).

***

If you start a blog, no matter what you end up writing about, make sure you keep it updated and post whenever you can (as long as you've spent time making the post good!). You never know who could be following your blog, and before you know it, you could have made a few new lifelong fans!

Want A Free Book? How About Two?

Thank you for reading this book! If you prefer ebooks, you can also get all three volumes in one ebook boxset.

The first book in my Little Forest paranormal mystery series, *The Former World*, is available for free from Amazon and other online bookstores, so why not check it out now?

If you sign up to my mailing list at www.jessicagracecoleman.com, you can also get the second in the series, *Memento Mori*, absolutely free, as well as the opportunity to hear about my new releases and exclusive Readers' Group competitions. How's that for a bargain?

If you've enjoyed this book, I'd really appreciate a review on Amazon, as reviews can really help independent authors like myself, thank you.

Acknowledgements

I'd like to say a big thank you to anyone who helped me (directly or indirectly) with these books. Special thanks go to James at GoOnWrite.com for the cover designs and Lauren K Nixon for her words on fanfiction.

About The Author

Jessica Grace Coleman was born in Stafford, England and raised in the nearby village of Little Haywood, a quaint English location that would later be remodelled into Beth Powers' home village in the Little Forest novels.

She studied Film Studies and American Studies at the University of Sussex in Brighton, and attended the University of Colorado at Boulder for a year as part of her course. A big fan of travelling, she has road tripped around North America and backpacked across China, South East Asia, Australia, and New Zealand.

Jessica has so far self-published five books in the Little Forest series: *The Former World*, *Memento Mori*, *The Exalted*, *Carnival Masquerade* and *The Gloaming*. She has also released her first short story collection, *Grown By The Wicked Moon*, featuring 14 weird and wonderful tales, as well as her non-fiction titles, *Creative Ways To Start Creative Writing, Volumes 1, 2 & 3*.

You can find out more about Jessica, her available books, and her works in progress at her website:

www.jessicagracecoleman.com and you can contact her at author@jessicagracecoleman.com. You can also sign up for her mailing list - where you'll be first to hear about her new releases and reader competitions - at www.jessicagracecoleman.com.

This is a Darker Times book - www.darkertimes.co.uk

Also Available from Jessica Grace Coleman

The Former World

A Little Forest Novel

Twenty-one year old Beth Powers is fed up with living in the tiny, gossip-fuelled village of Little Forest and resolves to escape to London with best friend, Veronica Summers. That is, until the body of Beth's colleague Emma Harris is found in the nearby woods, setting off the small community's well-oiled rumour mill.

Beth soon finds herself in the middle of a bizarre village conspiracy: was Emma's death really accidental? Why are Beth's nearest and dearest cutting her out of their lives? And what does it all have to do with the conveniently-timed arrival of handsome new resident, Connor Maguire?

Will Beth decide to leave her childhood home for good? And, more importantly, will Little Forest let her go?

The Former World (Little Forest Book One) is now available from Amazon and other online bookstores.

For more details, check out my site at www.jessicagracecoleman.com

Also Available from Jessica Grace Coleman

Memento Mori

A Little Forest Novel

Beth Powers is twenty-one, single, and lives in the traditional English village of Little Forest. She has a sister, a great group of friends, and a steady, if slightly boring, job. Oh, and she can see dead people.

Beth's home village isn't exactly normal, either, and a Memento Mori art exhibition showcasing Victorian photos of the dead is the catalyst for a whole new set of problems for the Little Forest Investigations team. Who was the dead woman who saved Beth's life last Hallowe'en? Why do spectres keep getting drawn to Beth's house? And what does it all have to do with the imprisoned murderer, Norman Carter?

Join Beth and the LFI gang in this Little Forest novel as they delve deeper into the Former World, seeking out spectres as they try and unlock the dark secrets surrounding their village, their lives, and their deaths.

Memento Mori (Little Forest Book Two) is now available from Amazon and other online bookstores.

For more details, check out my site at
www.jessicagracecoleman.com

Also Available from Jessica Grace Coleman

The Exalted

A Little Forest Novel

Beth Powers is twenty-one, single, and lives in the traditional English village of Little Forest. She has a sister, a great group of friends, and a steady, if slightly boring, job. Oh, and she can see dead people.

Along with the Little Forest Investigations team, Beth is on a mission to help the lost spectres that keep getting drawn back to Cherry Tree House, but as usual, it isn't all plain sailing.

Who was the leader of the brainwashing cult, 'The Exalted'? Why are residents of the village acting stranger than usual? And what does it all have to do with the events of 1921?

Join Beth and the LFI gang in this Little Forest novel as they explore myths, magic and mediums in their home village and try to discover the truth about the Former World.

The Exalted (Little Forest Book Three) is now available from Amazon and other online bookstores.

For more details, check out my site at www.jessicagracecoleman.com

Also Available from Jessica Grace Coleman

Carnival Masquerade

A Little Forest Novel

Beth Powers is twenty-one, single, and lives in the traditional English village of Little Forest. She has a sister, a great group of friends, and a steady, if slightly boring, job. Oh, and she can see dead people.

Like many other village residents, Beth is intrigued by the circus which has just set up shop on Willowton Common: 'Doctor Blackout's Magnificent Masquerade Carnival' is certainly bringing in the locals, but there's something not quite right about the whole set up, including the elusive Doctor Blackout himself.

Join Beth and the LFI gang in this Little Forest novel as they battle against the forces of evil, some bored spectres, and even one of their best friends. The Former World has never been so deadly.

Carnival Masquerade (Little Forest Book Four) is now available from Amazon and other online bookstores.

For more details, check out my site at www.jessicagracecoleman.com

Also Available from Jessica Grace Coleman

The Gloaming

A Little Forest Novel

Beth Powers is a pretty normal twenty-one year old woman. She has a sister, a great group of friends, and a steady – if slightly boring – job. She lives in the traditional English village of Little Forest. Oh, and she can see dead people.

When the Little Forest Investigations gang get a request from an Irish gazer in trouble, Connor jumps at the chance to go back to his homeland, and soon, the whole LFI team find themselves in rural Ireland. It's cute, it's quaint, and it's jam-packed full of dead people.

Join Beth and the rest of the LFI gang in this Little Forest novel as they continue their quest to help the spectres of the Former World, dealing with madmen, witches, and unwanted visitors on the way.

The Gloaming (Little Forest Book Five) is now available from Amazon and other online bookstores.

For more details, check out my site at
www.jessicagracecoleman.com

Also Available from Jessica Grace Coleman

Grown By The Wicked Moon

A Short Story Collection

'Grown By The Wicked Moon' is the first short story collection from Staffordshire writer Jessica Grace Coleman (author of the Little Forest series of mystery novels), and features 14 weird and wonderful tales.

This book delves into the dark lives (and deaths) of a wide range of characters, with a little bit of horror, a dash of fantasy and a pinch of humour thrown in for good measure. It will take you from a seemingly doomed girl lost in the woods to a disturbing business transaction, from a writer whose made up characters are a little *too* realistic to a spurned woman on a mission, from a mysterious hero in a small town to a bored ghost who finds out that death isn't all it's cracked up to be.

All of these tales have elements of darkness in them, and all of them were written on cold, gloomy, wintry evenings, where they were cultivated under the steady gaze of the black night sky. These stories were grown by the wicked moon.

For more details, check out my site at
www.jessicagracecoleman.com